HACKING WALL STREET

Attacks and Countermeasures

Karlos Krinklebine

Hacking Wall Street

January 30, 2009

Hacking Wall Street – Attacks and Countermeasures by K. Krinklebine

ISBN - 10: 1-44146-363-1

ISBN - 13: 978-1-44146-363-0

First Printing

10 9 8 7 6 5 4 3 2 1

In memory of my sister
Deborah

Acknowledgements

As with any book, this book could not have been written without the help of many people. There are so many people I could thank. I will name a few of the people that brought me to the place where I am today and ultimately gave me the ability to build this tome.

Thank you to Dan Geer, for the forward in this book, suggestions, and for reading early copy that quite frankly shouldn't have been read by anyone with any command of the English language.

Special thanks to James Kelley for correcting what I thought was English and then taking those handicapped drafts and translating them into something the rest of planet Earth could clearly understand.

I would like to thank my son, Damien for allowing his daddy to burn many weekends at the computer keyboard writing this book. And last but not least, I'd like to thank my wife, Hile. Being married to me can't be easy.

Foreword

It is my privilege to say a few words about this book, words I mean more as an aperitif rather than a tasting sample.

Financial services firms were the first non-military sector to pay attention to information security. They have long been, and are likely to remain, the avatar for all other civilian sectors. If you look at finance, you can generally see the future. There are several reasons why this is so.

While the first is the most pertinent it is perhaps the least relevant -- banks are where the money is. But money does not make money unless it moves, and so move it does. The bigger the bank, the greater the percentage of its business is done with other banks, an oddity not found in other industries (Ford does not buy and sell GM cars) with the minor exception of some small parts of the energy market. The chief trading partners for major financial houses are other major financial houses, thus predisposing banks to take digital security seriously -- their counterparties are also their competitors.

What banks buy and sell is risk, which likewise predisposes them to understand risk or, more correctly, to engage in risk management. Risk management is inherently forward looking, as best said by Borge: "The purpose of risk management is to change the future, not to explain the past." Changing the future is hard, but somebody has to do it and, as always, two things help -- a prepared mind and good cash flow. Banks have both.

Finally, banks have and do pay attention to digital security because they don't actually make widgets or even stockpile widgets; they move bits. While bits are bits, some bits are more important than others and bits are not naturally self-protecting. When the system is digital, its failures are binary.

Paleobiologists like Gould see evolution as "punctuated equilibria" which is to say long periods of stability interrupted by short periods of rapid change. Evolution, as they describe it, is not some steady upslope at 8% grade, but rather the unexpected when least expected and then a flurry of change that will eventually damp itself out enough to be called progress, as if anything that brought us to where we are must have been progress since this is the best world yet made.

The risk management we need might therefore be understood as (1)the ability to maximize the damping effects of stable periods of risk and (2) to be prepared to handle the punctuating events of the definitively unpredictable, the latter being what Taleb famously called a "black swan."

Can we look back and see a few of these sorts of episodic catharses? Of course we can. Every transformation of the computing world has been a surprise, one that removed the reason for existence upon which its predecessor depended and which was later superseded in like manner whatever followed. The first computers were rare, expensive, and they made redundant legions of folks who once worked out tables of logarithms to nine digits by hand. Time share destroyed the market for stand-alone behemoths, and desktop PCs destroyed the market for time share. Today, software as a service (SaaS) looks poised to destroy the desktop PC. At each stage, the best X ever produced was also the last X ever produced as it was itself rendered irrelevant by the leading edge of the next phase. As the son of an accountant, I saw this first hand; my father had the finest Frieden mechanical desk calculator made, it was mechanically programmable -- a thing of beauty -- and yet the lousy Bowmar Brain made mechanical desk calculators irrelevant. You can surely name example after example of the same phenomenon -- that of a kind of equilibrium punctuated by the end of the environment on which the most evolved members of that environment depended.

To the biome, to the occupier of a niche that was here yesterday and will be gone tomorrow, change is a surprise. No tree can say "Time to move" and no salamander can think "I need to evolve." Evolutionary change depends on this unpredictability; otherwise yesterday's winners are tomorrow's winners, yesterday's dominant species only get more dominant tomorrow. As Grove said, only the paranoid survive.

Note that "change" is not a synonym for "disaster." Just as some pines have cones that only open after they've been burned in a forest fire, opportunism as a counter to disaster is something we can see in our world -- today and every day -- in that for every backdoor some worm or virus installs, you can bet your paycheck some other bit of malware is soon searching for the self-same backdoor for its own purposes. A backdoor unused is like a biological niche unoccupied; Nature, both biologic and digital, abhors a vacuum -- that backdoor will get used, the only question being by whom or what.

In the natural world, a high presence of attack pressure must and does result in a high rate of mutation. What part of your body suffers the most daily insults and thus mutates all day, every day? The E. coli in your gut. Their mutation rate rises and falls in relation to stress since if things are going well a mutation is likely to be deleterious whereas if things are going badly it may well be a last chance and, in any case, reproductive fidelity is more metabolically expensive than producing mutations. A withering digital attack ought to provoke some adaptive mutations in the target whether we are talking of a single executable or an industrial sector. Put differently, if you are losing a game you cannot afford to lose, try changing the rules.

I define complexity as the density of feedback loops. A lot of people say that complexity is the enemy of security -- I'm one of them -- but at the same time I am here to argue that we have to learn from Nature precisely because Nature is the most complex "thing" we will ever see. Nature is an existence proof that complexity is not the enemy of life, but complexity is the enemy of stasis. Our problem is that we've pretty much equated security with stasis, and it is slowly getting us into trouble. Take forest fires -- if you always quench them, such as to protect vacation homes and tourist dollars, then you necessarily build up the supply of unburned fuel wood in the ecosystem and someday you get a much bigger fire. If you let any and every fire burn, someone who can vote will lose. If you prevent any and every fire, you look smart and life goes on, and predictably so... until it doesn't.

If we look at Nature in the form of the equations of ecology, we see two alternative games for survival, r-selection and K-selection. R-selected species produce many offspring, each of whom has a relatively low probability of surviving to adulthood. By contrast, K-selected species are strong competitors in crowded niches, and invest more heavily in much fewer offspring, each of whom has a relatively high probability of surviving to adulthood. If we change the term from "produce many offspring" to "re-image frequently" you now have precisely the advice Microsoft's D'Anseglio gave when he said, "[In] dealing with rootkits and advanced spyware programs, the only solution is to rebuild from scratch. In some cases, there really is no way to recover without nuking the systems from orbit." This brilliant remark is a direct, if inadvertent, suggestion that desktop machines need to be r-selected, i.e., they need to die and be re-born often. If you are of a mind to invest in virtual machines, you may get r-selection as a side effect to whatever it is that you are trying to do with VMs.

I trace the security industry as we know it today to one of Gould's punctuations appearing as one of Taleb's black swan events, but one in relatively slow motion compared to, say, the Witty worm. Specifically, I trace the birth of the industry in which most readers earn your keep to Microsoft's introduction of a TCP/IP stack as a freebie in the Windows platform. Besides putting FTP Software out of business, a tactic followed so many times that I have literally lost count, the TCP/IP stack took an OS designed for a single owner/operator on a private net, if networked at all, and connected it to the world. Once that stack was installed by default, every sociopath became your next door neighbor and, as such, we can point to that event as the birth of our industry, confirmed by a sudden, one-time-only, wholly dramatic spike in that second derivative of the rate of attacks reported to the CERT immediately following that appearance of a TCP/IP stack on Windows. Note that I said a spike in the second derivative; nothing much else happened for a bit but, similarly, lighting the solid fuel on the Space Shuttle doesn't have any instantaneously visible effect either.

The second of these equilibrium punctuating moments occurred, as far as I can tell, some time around 24 months ago. Like the first, it was no thunderbolt, more like a glacier finishing its slide across a river bed and thus "suddenly" damming the waters. This moment was when our principal opponents changed over from adventurers and braggarts to professionals. In a sense, professionalization of the attack class is akin to virulence in that the increasing immunity of computer systems forced an upgrade in the ability of the attacker to attack, i.e., finding vulnerabilities and exploiting them is now hard enough that it has moved out of the realm of being a hobby and into the realm of being a job. This changes several things, notably that hobbyists confirm their successes with public kills and share their findings so as to claim the bragging rights in which they are paid, whereas professionals do not share and are paid in something more liquid than fame. Speaking biologically, a mutation (toward strength) on the part of the prey was matched by a mutation (also toward strength) on the part of the predator. As a side effect, the fraction of all vulnerabilities that are unknown has risen and will continue to rise.

We have yet to reach the post-punctuation equilibrium in this cycle. The mutation toward strength represented by professionalization of the attack class was not a simple, compensating match for the increasing self-protection in merchant operating systems. It went further and it did so because, at least for the first world, the digital arena is now clearly where the opportunities are, such as that when robbing banks it is the amateur who uses a hand gun and the professional who uses a bot.

In the fall of 2006, I did some back of the envelope calculations that resulted in a guess that 15-30% of all desktops had some degree of external control present. I got a bit of hate mail over that, but in the intervening months Cerf said 20-40%, Microsoft said 66%, and IDG said 75%. It doesn't matter which is right; what matters is that this changes a core feature of the ecosystem -- and changing a core feature is the very definition of a punctuating event.

In this case, it actually was not standing up a professional class of attackers any more than in the first go 'round it was a spike in the second derivative of the reported attack rate. What it was, was that a fundamental assumption of network security has now been breached and there is no putting it back together again.

Ever since we did Kerberos, the idea has been "I'm OK and you're OK, but the network between us cannot be trusted for a second." Authentication, authorization, and accountability all begin with authentication and that, in turn, begins by asking the Operating System the name of the user. What has really changed is that it is no longer true that "I'm OK and you're OK" since it is entirely likely that the counterparty to whom you are connecting is already compromised. A secure network connection? Who cares if the other end is hosed? Spafford was right but early when he likened network security to hiring an armored car to deliver gold bars from someone living in a cardboard box to someone sleeping on a park bench.

That is the new security situation you and we are facing -- what to do about 0wned counterparties. This is a today issue, not a tomorrow issue; the November 2006 10-Q filing for E-Trade included a material loss due to exactly this problem, the first SEC filing of this sort to my knowledge. 0wned machines mean key loggers and key loggers mean opponents who can get you to help them in the pump phase of a pump & dump stock fraud, whether you like it or not. If and when you ever bother to call your broker to complain that this or that purchase was not one you did, the broker has two choices: "You are an idiot." or "We'll make it up to you." Such a situation is untenable, and indicative of the need to evolve.

If, by chance, you think the professionals aren't winning, just consider that they now value stealth over persistence, i.e., they find it so easy to 0wn machines that they make no effort to survive reboot, preferring instead to hide in-core only. Consider this the equivalent of gene therapy as prescribed by Dr. Faustus.

At the end of the day, however, we are facing a much bigger, more metaphysical question than the few so far posed. The bigger question is this: How much security do we want?

How much security do we want is the real question, and while Nature can give us more clues than we can ever use to improving what we puny humans can do, we are fast closing on a point where the question we must ask is whether we wish to turn over our security to sentient machines. Within the career lifetime of nearly everyone reading this Foreword, computers will be smarter than we are. Security is already the most difficult intellectual profession on the planet. The core knowledge base has reached the point where new recruits can no longer hope to be competent generalists, serial specialization is the only broad option available to them. Computers will soon be called upon to do what we cannot, and that is to protect us from other computers, and to ask no permission in so doing. Every practitioner can tell some story where an insane affection for convenience caused people for whom you were nominally responsible to create, or at least tolerate, insecurity and to be offended if you endeavored to make them see that light.

The next punctuation of the equilibrium will therefore be the effective end of the general purpose computer as a consumer durable -- as presaged by Apple dropping the word "Computer" from its name or leading Wall Street trading firms already going back to displays only on the desktop and no PCs at all. Software as a Service, or temporary periods of invasive remote-control of the client-side machine by the server-side counterparty, or apps on hand-helds that only run because they are perpetually connected to back-end processing -- all of these are the leading edge of the next equilibrium punctuatum. Yet, if you do not have a general purpose computer, with which, to paraphrase Felten, you have the freedom to tinker, then I ask you what kind of security will that be?

Karlos Krinklebine, in inviting me to write this Foreword, proves Gibson's idea that the future is already here, just unevenly distributed. Krinklebine shows you that the second epoch of information security is over and he and his colleagues are well into the third. The tour of the combination battlefield and sausage factory which follows this Foreword asks many of the questions that are part of this next moment of punctuation, the ones that derivatively follow professionalization of the opponents and which will soon endeavor to make the general purpose computer less general. He is a front-line soldier in the war, and war is hell. He knows what he is talking about and, which is more, he, too, hates the circumstances that make the distasteful necessary and the necessary distasteful.

Much more than myself, he is showing you how the sausage is made. He is walking the perimeter of the financial services network world with you so that you can judge not so much the how of what must now come but rather the why. "Why" is the only real source of power, without it we are powerless, and you would be well advised to pay attention. Lamport's witticism, that "A distributed system is one on which I cannot get any work done because some machine I have never heard of has crashed" is even more true of that most distributed of all digital systems, financial services. Though Krinklebine apologizes for the occasional technicality he must describe, no apology is needed unless, of course, you don't want to know "why" or even "how," you only want to be protected. That has never been a good bargain for a sentient being, but then again only a sentient being will likely read this book, or want to. My compliments to you for getting this far.

Daniel E. Geer, Jr., Sc.D.

April 2008

Table of Contents

Introduction

This book is about online fraud. Specifically, it is about fraud in the online brokerage industry. The focus on brokerage notwithstanding, this book applies equally to any company conducting business on the Internet today. The attacks and techniques used by cyber criminals are similar, if not identical to, the attacks you will experience in your own industry. Fortunately, the suggestions and solutions in this book are similarly applicable.

This book ultimately attempts to cover a lot of ground in as brief a book as possible. The author certainly could have expanded this into an immense paperweight, but in the end the meat of the book would have been obstructed by the sheer volume of information. While every attempt was made to keep this book as non-technical as possible, it was necessary in certain sections to resort to the esoteric language of high-technology.

We will start this book with a brief summary of the online brokerage industry and the core issues impacting the industry today. We will then round the discussion out with some analysis of the malware targeting the industry. At the end we will look at various products and solutions built to solve the problems presented.

Inevitably, some readers of this book may quickly come to the incorrect conclusion that this is a how-to book for the budding cyber criminal. Unfortunately, while the author of this book would love to claim all of this material is new and cutting edge, a very large portion of this information is already known to the cyber criminal community.

This book serves also as an educational tool to those that are typically not aware of the big picture. This larger audience may include the corporate security, compliance, and fraud departments at your company.

The aim of this book, then, is to help everyone understand the history of the problem, understand the current situation and understand what the future holds in store. With this understanding, your company can implement defensive strategies to help thwart all but the most skilled cyber criminals.

CHAPTER 1 An Introduction to Online Trading

Technology... is a queer thing. It brings you great gifts with one hand, and it stabs you in the back with the other.

- C.P. Snow

There is a well known story, actually a legend, that Joseph Kennedy sold all his stock the day before catastrophic collapse of the US stock market in 1929. Unlike the apocryphal Mr. Kennedy, most investors lost huge amounts of money in the crash that began the Great Depression. As the story goes, Joseph Kennedy received a stock tip from a shoe shine boy, during the time when the stock market was the arena of the rich and powerful. Joseph Kennedy decided that if a common person could own stock, there must be something very wrong with the market and proceeded to sell his positions.[1]

Today, billions upon billions of securities are traded everyday in marketplaces around the globe. No longer do you need to be rich and powerful, nor do you need a personal broker to participate in the market. All you need is a computer, some money, and a decent financial history to trade to your heart's content. The markets have truly become accessible to the masses.

With the proliferation of computer technology, corporations have greatly benefited from the automation of tasks, allowing more work to be done by fewer employees. They continue to benefit as processing power, storage and Internet bandwidth grow at a staggering pace. Automation has

---

1. CBRonline. "Ecommerce: Who wants to be a millionaire." CBRonline. http://www.cbronline.com/article_cbr.asp?guid=45E2E90F-060B-4661-BFC7-9931211A4FCF.

allowed the average worker to produce at a far greater level than previously thought possible.

With the fast pace of life in the 21st century, people have demanded the same automation of mundane tasks to allow them more free time. The digital age is touching almost every aspect of our lives, some examples include:

- Automated teller machines (ATMs) service the majority of your banking needs
- Bar codes link purchased items to backend systems that track price, stock levels and buying patterns
- Automated gasoline pumps allow you to speed through the service station
- Online shopping lets you literally buy anything you want, any time of the day, from anywhere in the world
- Corporate networks allow you to share data quickly and efficiently with your co-workers, allowing you to be more productive

What is ironic is that the exponential growth in computer resources has also allowed the criminal element, at least those skilled in the arts, to expand. Today's cyber criminal not only steals more with less risk than ever before, but also shares the necessary techniques and resources with others. Since the introduction of securities trading, there has always been a criminal element looking to manipulate this marketplace to make a quick buck. Now, the modern criminal no longer needs to be physically present to rob you, for the modern criminal now lurks in the shadows of the Internet.

Today, trading stocks online has never been easier; in the first quarter of 2008 more than 10 million people will have bought or sold some form of investment online. Additionally, the rate that new users are getting onto the Internet, opening brokerage accounts, and trading securities online continues to grow at a staggering pace (Figure 1-1).

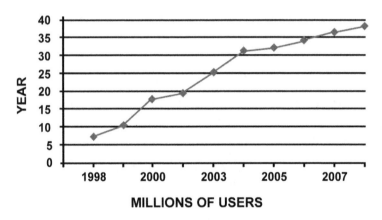

Figure 1-1 Growth of Online Brokerage

While 38 million online brokerage accounts may seem like a large number, when you compare it to the 238 million Internet users in North America alone, or the 1.4 billion Internet users worldwide, you can expect that this number is capable of explosive growth.[2]

The tremendous growth of over 600% in the past decade coupled with the potential for further growth, has attracted cyber criminals intent on exploiting the online financial services arena. Enabled by the efficient, inexpensive, and often anonymous access the Internet provides, these criminals have engaged in unauthorized transactions worth billions of dollars as part of a fast-growing new form of online fraud.[3] In turn, their activities have triggered investigations by federal authorities. While cyber criminals will go after any company of any size providing any form of product or service, the focus of this book is on online brokerage accounts.

Cyber fraud is not only thriving on the Internet, it is also becoming one of the biggest challenges facing online brokers today. According to the Federal Bureau of Investigation's (FBI) Internet Fraud Complaint Center (IFCC) and the Department of Justice (DOJ), Internet fraud involving stock information is the second most common form of investment fraud, amounting to over $10 billion dollars a year in losses.[4] The Securities and Exchange Com-

---

2. Miniwatts Marketing Group. "Internet World Stats Usage and Population
Statistics," Internet Coaching Library,
http://www.internetworldstats.com/stats.htm (accessed April 10, 2008).

3. Federal Bureau of Investigations, "Financial Crimes Report To The Public Fiscal Year 2006," Federal Bureau of Investigations, Washington, DC, March, 2007.

4. Fowler, B., Franklin, C., Hyde, R. ""Internet Securities Fraud: Old Trick, New Medium." Duke Law & Technology Review, (February 28, 2001),
http://www.law.duke.edu/journals/dltr/articles/2001dltr0006.html.

mission (SEC) receives several hundred complaints a day about suspected online fraud, up from a handful only a few years ago. The agency now faces a staggering number of cyber fraud complaints and inquiries on a daily basis. This congestion further reduces the risk to the cyber criminal of ever being caught.

Cyber fraud in the financial services industry is growing at a staggering pace, much faster than public awareness of it. The fraud is being fed by the rising use of the Internet for personal finance coupled with the easy availability of snooping software that allows hackers to steal personal account information. Federal regulators cited recent cases in which cyber criminals gained access to customer accounts, through the use of credential stealing software, at several large online brokers and then used the customers' funds to buy large quantities of specific stock securities. By carefully planning this theft, the cyber criminals were able to drive up share prices so they could sell those stocks at a profit. In the past few years, online brokerage account intrusions have markedly increased. Though it should be noted that intrusions into all forms of Internet accounts have also risen.

A major online broker, the nation's fourth-largest, has stated in their 10-k filings that in 2006 alone they lost in excess of $31 million dollars to fraud. Most of the broker's losses occurred through "concerted rings" located in Eastern Europe and Thailand. These rings were responsible for $18 million in losses in the third quarter of 2006 alone.[5]

Not one single large firm has been spared, and recent research shows that this issue is now trickling down to smaller brokerage firms. With more than 5,100 brokerage firms in the United States alone, many Internet accessible, the cyber criminals have a large number of targets. It is important to realize that the size of the cyber fraud in general, as expected, is much larger than just the financial services fraud numbers.

Today, roughly 80% of Americans that use the Internet routinely conduct online financial transactions such as stock transactions, online banking or filing taxes.[6] There were almost nine million online fraud/identity thefts in 2006 alone, with losses for that year reaching a staggering $56 billion dollars.[7] The average loss per identity fraud incident was around $6,400 dollars.[8] As one would expect, approximately 84% of Americans using the Internet are concerned that they could become a victim of online fraud.[9] Two-thirds of those who conduct

5. Nakashima, Ellen. "Hackers Zero in on Online Stock Accounts." Washington Post (October 24, 2006), http://www.washington-post.com/wp?dyn/content/article/2006/10/23/AR2006102301257.html.

6. National Cyber Security Alliance and Bank of America. "Online Fraud Report." Staysafeonline.org. http://staysafeonline.org/news/onlinefraudreportfinal.pdf.

7. TNS, The VeriSign Secured Seal Research Review, Report, Aug. 2006.

8. Javelin Strategy and Research and the Better Business Bureau, 2006 Identity Fraud Survey Report, January 2006.

personal or financial transactions are concerned about having hackers steal financial information from their computers.[10] Studies have shown that up to 50% of users on the Internet today will avoid making future purchases online out of their fear of having their financial information stolen. Furthermore, 49% of those surveyed, who were concerned about a loss of their personal data, would not make a purchase at all.[11] To believe that this problem hasn't landed squarely on your company's doorstep is to be burying one's proverbial head in the sand.[12]

Ultimately the issue is not just yours, even if your firm isn't yet a victim, large increases in fraud could cause permanent damage to the financial services industry and the markets. With such a large number of users trading online, fear could remove those players from the market, leading ultimately to less volume for all firms.

---

9. TNS, The VeriSign Secured Seal Research Review, Report, Aug. 2006.

10. National Cyber Security Alliance and Bank of America. "Online Fraud Report." Staysafeonline.org. http://staysafeonline.org/news/onlinefraudreportfinal.pdf.

11. Cyber Security Industry Alliance, "Internet Security National Survey, No. 3," Cyber Security Industry Alliance, Arlington, VA, May 23, 2006.

12. Kruszelnicki, Karl S. "Ostrich Head in Sand." ABC Online. http://www.abc.net.au/science/k2/moments/s1777947.htm (accessed April 10, 2008).

Terms

ATM – Automated Teller Machine. An ATM, also commonly called a MAC machine, is a computerized device that provides customers access to financial accounts without human assistance.

BJA – Bureau of Justice Assistance. The BJA is an organization dedicated to the reduction and prevention of crimes, violence and drug abuse and to improve the functioning of the criminal justice system.

DOJ – Department of Justice. The United States federal department responsible for enforcing federal laws.

FBI – Federal Bureau of Investigations. A United States federal law enforcement department that is the principal investigative unit of the Department of Justice.

IFCC – Internet Fraud Complaint Center. Now the IC3, the Internet Crime Complain Center, it is a partnership between the FBI, the NW3C and the BJA. It provides a centralized reporting mechanism for reporting Internet crime and acts as a clearing house for law enforcement and regulatory bodies at the state, federal and international level.

NW3C – National White Collar Crime Center. The NW3C is a congressionally-funded organization that equips state and local law enforcement agencies with the skills and resources needed to tackle emerging economic and cyber crime problems through a combination of training and support services.

SEC –Securities and Exchange Commission. The SEC's role is to protect investors and maintain fair, orderly and efficient markets. This organization enforces federal security laws and regulates the securities industry.

CHAPTER 2 Security at the 30,000 ft View

Strategy without tactics is the slowest route to victory. Tactics without strategy is the noise before defeat.

- Sun Tzu

The Sun Tzu quote at the beginning of this chapter rings so true for client security and security in general. While a clear strategic vision is important, you must also combine it with numerous tactical initiatives to keep the cyber criminals at bay. Failure to incorporate a tactical program will cause not only continuing financial losses, but it may actually keep you from ever completing a strategic vision. Ideally, you want to keep pushing your attacker around, forcing him to innovate and expend resources while you execute your strategic vision. Applying constantly changing pressure allows you to determine the capability of your attackers while eliminating distracting chaff. After all, it's easy to eliminate the low hanging fruit; however the really good attackers eventually encapsulate their knowledge into easy to use tool kits. So your tactical program will take care of a lot of the "noise" while your strategic program will put large burdens on the most skilled attackers. Using a combination of strategic and tactical programs, you will maximize your return.

In order to get you, the reader, into thinking about strategic and tactical programs, we need to first introduce you to some basic rules. Before we begin, the author would like to remind you that this book is not a substitute for a proper client security program; however, the author would be doing a great disservice to you, if he didn't start off by explaining some basic axioms of security. We will then follow that brief conversation with one that discusses the economics of client security. Cli-

ent security at its very core is no different than the
security of anything else. What you need to do is
understand how to apply the basic principals to
secure your systems at a reasonable cost. This
chapter occurs early in the book because you
should always be thinking of how to thwart the
attacker through the application of these basic
principals. Below is listed a short list of axioms to
apply to client security.

There is no perfect security solution

This first item is not only straightforward, but
of little surprise; given unlimited resources any
security solution can be breached. You shouldn't
just give up, however. The goal of any security
solution is not to be flawless, but simply to make
the resources required to breach the target high
enough to the attacker that it deters most, if not all,
attackers from trying to breach the target. Alternatively, the resource cost can drive the attacker to a
weaker target, preferably another company.
Resources can include any combination of time,
effort, money and the increased risk of being
caught and prosecuted.

Consider, for example, a bank. Banks employ
large amounts of security but still get robbed.
Bank employees still attempt to embezzle funds.
Banks still deal with fraud on a daily basis. Banks,
however, are not about to go out of business; they
are aware of which security measures cost effec-

tively deter criminals and accept a roughly predictable loss that the business can write off or cover through an insurance policy. The same is true with the Internet. Just because it acts more like a virtual entity doesn't mean the axiom doesn't apply.

Not convinced? Here's another example. Nuclear missile launch codes are very well protected. The briefcase that contains the nuclear launch codes, known affectionately as the Nuclear Football, is one of the most secure systems in existence. It follows the president everywhere, and is carried by an armed officer with orders to shoot to kill. The simple rule is that the football is to be near the President at all times when he is away from the White House. It sounds easy doesn't it? Presidents Gerald Ford, Jimmy Carter, George H.W. Bush and Bill Clinton have all accidentally left the Nuclear Football behind.[13,14] Even more embarrassing, Jimmy Carter once left the nuclear launch codes in one of his suits when it was sent to the dry cleaner.[15] If one had enough resources, it would have been possible to acquire the Nuclear Football during one of these incidents. Fortunately that never happened.

---

13. Pullella, Philip. "Bush's Nuclear 'Football' in Vatican Hallowed Halls." Reuters (June 4, 2004), http://www.signonsandiego.com/news/world/20040604-0731-pope-bush-football.html.

14. Unknown. "World: Americas Clinton Drops Nuclear Football." BBC News Website. http://news.bbc.co.uk/2/hi/americas/328442.stm (accessed March 18, 2008).

15. Ibid

If untouched, all security solutions weaken over time

You may not want to hear this, but it is a simple matter of fact. As computing power increases, security solutions tend to fail. It's not that they are bad security solutions; it's just that when they are built, they address issues of the day using the computing power available. Encryption is a great example. Decades ago, the data encryption standard known as DES was developed. DES allowed for a 56-bit key. In English, that means that a brute force attempt at decryption would have to try up to 2^{56} possible keys. At the time, the fastest supercomputer was the Cray-1 which was capable of roughly 160 million operations per second. The Cray-1 contained 8 megabytes of memory[16] which was woefully inadequate for breaking DES encryption. Not to mention it cost over $8 million dollars. Key length is always a tradeoff since longer key lengths requires more computing power to encrypt and decrypt. Ultimately, you try to make the key length long enough to prevent brute forcing for the foreseeable future but not so long that it becomes computationally slow. The optimal security solution will take into account the life of the secret and the amount of time it takes for an attacker to defeat your solution.

16. Cray Inc. http://www.cray.com/about_cray/history.html.

By the time the mid-nineties hit, it was widely believed that the National Security Agency (NSA) could brute force DES keys. By 1998, a custom piece of hardware was developed that could brute force keys at a rate of 92 billion keys per second, leading to the cracking of a piece of encrypted text in 56 hours.[17] Today's latest encryption standard, Advanced Encryption Standard (AES), and its 128-bit key, is assumed to be safe from brute forcing. Even a 128-bit key, however, doesn't eliminate the possibility of someone finding short cuts to defeat the algorithm. What this history ultimately means to you is that you must continuously evolve your security controls just to maintain your current level of security. If you wish to move your security forward, then you must expend resources to keep your security level where it is, *and* expend additional resources to move it forward.

If given a chance an attacker will go around your security rather than through it

Security actually works and the bad guys know it, which is why they look for gaps. Attackers will always attempt to exploit a gap before they need to take on your security controls. For instance, if you build your house out of steel, but

---

17. Cryptography Research. "Record Breaking DES Key Search Completed." Cryptography Research. http://www.cryptography.com/resources/whitepapers/DES.html (February 12, 2008).

leave the front door open, a burglar will walk right in rather than attempting to breach the skin of the house. The attacker, given the choice, will always attempt to go around your security, not through it. If you have a great security program, then it's likely the attacker will find no easy workarounds and will have to go through it. At this point, the advantage becomes yours.

Your security is as good as the weakest link

Assuming you were successful with your security program, and have holes too small to exploit, the attacker must confront your security head on. If that occurs, the attacker will always take the path of least resistance in an attempt to bypass your controls and detection. When evaluating your security system, you should make sure to take the human element into consideration as it is often the chink in your armor.

Defense in depth and diversity

You may have heard the term *defense in depth* before. On the surface, this phrasing is flawed. Depth alone will not secure you. Case in point, using a simplified argument, a 2-tier application architecture typically requires a firewall between the Internet and the web server, and a firewall between the web server and the database server. If one applies the defense in depth axiom, then it is okay to buy identical firewalls from the same vendor and place them at the specified locations. Now let's step back for a second and analyze that assumption. If a cyber criminal is able to exploit your edge firewall, then one can infer that the internal firewall will fall almost instantaneously to the same exploit that penetrated the edge firewall. A diversity component would make sure that the firewalls were from two separate vendors. Diversity results in higher internal maintenance costs, but greatly increases security.

The concept of defense in depth and diversity allows for flawed security solutions. As we all know, any computer program has flaws, including security software. Because flaws exist, you layer security solutions so that if one layer fails to stop that attacker, there is a chance another layer will protect you. In order for an attacker to succeed, he must bypass all layers successfully. One way to think of it is to assume a security solution is a piece of Swiss cheese. First you want to find slices with the smallest number of holes. Then you want to layer slices so that the holes don't line up. If you can do that, then you have a pretty good set of security products in place.

Security must be balanced against costs and convenience

Security costs time, effort, and money, and it should be balanced against what you are protecting. You would never buy a $400 safe to protect a single dollar since the costs of doing so is greater than the value of the protected asset. Nor would you invest in a $5 million dollar security program if your losses are $10,000 a year. A general rule of thumb is that if you have had no security incidents then you are likely spending too much, and if the cost of clean up is costing you more than you are spending then you are likely spending too little. Unfortunately, there is a huge gap between the two extremes, and finding the perfect sweet spot requires not only skill, but a little luck, too.

Additionally, security typically comes with a convenience cost. This cost is due to the fact that by its very definition, security is an attempt to make some resource harder to access. Typically, it will require your users to provide some level of interaction, annoying your customers and causing some level of turnover. Great security solutions are transparent, and often incorporated into the design of a web site or product at the onset. The reality is that most security solutions are shoe-horned in when problems appear, at times when transparency usually isn't an option.

Client security is a business issue not a security issue

Everyone loves to call client security a security issue because people like to turn the issues into technical problems with technical solutions. While the end state may or may not be a technical issue, the initial decision is really a risk management discussion. Risk management concerns are really business concerns, not security issues. It is up to the business owner or risk management team to determine how to accept the risk. Options include avoiding the risk, reducing the risk, accepting the risk, or transferring the risk. Risk avoidance is accomplished by either not performing the activity causing the risk, which in most cases of client security isn't possible, or by eliminating it via some process or technology. Risk reduction allows for the event to occur, but uses controls to reduce the severity of the loss. Acceptance is exactly that - it accepts the loss. Companies generally choose acceptance when the cost of mitigating the loss is greater over time than the loss itself. Risk transfer moves the risk to another party. In client security, risk transfer typically takes the form of insurance policies or it may mean sharing the loss with the customer.

Keep it simple

Although last, this axiom is the most important of this chapter. Keeping your design simple can't be stressed enough. While the technologies you deploy may be far from simple, the logical flow on how all the moving parts interact should be easily understandable. If you build something really complex, then it's hard to understand, which makes it hard to explain, which makes it even harder to audit. Once you arrive at that level of complexity, you lose the ability to attribute cost savings to any of the parts. What's worse is that gaps may exist that you are not aware of and layering another technology may or may not fix the issue. What is certain is that your design will now have another degree of complexity, and be even harder to understand and maintain. Attackers will ultimately exploit this ambiguity.

Now that the basic rules are in place, the next question that always follows is "How much do I spend?" Countermeasure selection and the resulting return on investment (ROI) calculations are often a difficult topic. There are literally hundreds of products on the market, and there often isn't any solid data on the effectiveness of a given product. To make matters worse, it becomes extremely difficult to calculate residual risk after you have deployed multiple products. This problem is due to two main reasons: firstly, products often have overlapping feature sets, and secondly, they tend to strengthen or weaken the features of other products. Another issue develops from subtle changes in how the countermeasure is deployed. Small configuration choices can result in huge swings in effectiveness, and therefore savings.

One good example of this snowball effect is the deployment of enhanced authentication systems, such as those sold by RSA and VeriSign and other vendors. Enhanced authentication is simply the asking of a knowledge based question when certain data points cross a threshold, which indicates that there may be an increased risk associated with executing a transaction with this user on his current device. Let us assume that your deployment consists of four challenge questions. When an event crosses your predefined threshold, you prompt the user with a question she must answer to gain access; some companies prompt the user with two questions and require only one be successfully answered. Now let us assume that our user traveled to a public kiosk and the challenge question was compromised. If your firm asks one question, the attacker has compromised it and has a one-in-four chance of getting the question he knows the answer to. If your firm asks two questions, then the attacker has two chances to gain entry. He has a one-in-four chance to get the question he knows. He also has a one-in-four chance of getting a question that he's had time to research. Overall, the attacker has a fifty-fifty shot at gaining entry.

When looking at the micro scale, this minor difference doesn't seem to be a big deal. At the macro level, however, there are huge differences. Let us assume that in a one month period an attacker can gather 100 users' question/answer credentials. Assuming that the questions displayed are chosen at random, the firm that displays one question has allowed the attacker into about 25 accounts, while the firm with two questions displayed has let the attacker into approximately 50 accounts. The second firm will have double the losses as the first firm assuming no other controls are in place. This difference is due to the simple requirement of displaying two questions instead of one.

Now let us take this example one step further with something that isn't mentioned by either vendor. Do you keep track of when a question is used on a public computer versus a private computer? Let us assume firm two, the one displaying two questions, does track this information and that firm one does not. Let us also assume that firm two will not reuse a question that was displayed and answered on a public computer until all the other questions have been through a rotation. This step essentially takes a question out of rotation until the other questions have been "burned" by public computer use. Now the tables have turned - the first firm still has a one-in-four chance of the attacker getting a compromised question. The second firm has reduced their risk; the attacker will not even have a chance of getting a compromised question until the user has burned all his other questions on public computers.

In addition, recording public versus private use provides firm two with quite a bit of intelligence. For instance, if users are getting compromised after "burning" their questions on public comput-

ers, company two might require users to reset their
passwords after all their questions have been used
on public terminals. The company might also
want the user to select new questions. Company
one, however, will not know if they are being compromised by malware on a user's personal computer or by the use of public terminals. Company
one's system will likely lose effectiveness more
quickly than company two. At the very least, company two will know the source of the losses and be
able to plan for an effective countermeasure.

These scenarios are simplified versions of what
you will typically run into. Understanding the
nuances of your decisions will take some time and
effort. Making decisions without knowing their
impact is possibly the worst thing you can do. You
should not rush security decisions. Always understand the impact of your decisions at not only the
micro level, but at the macro level.

Understanding the Fraud Curve

In the 1962 book, *Diffusion of Innovations*, Ever-
ett M. Rogers theorized that innovation spreads
through a society in an S-curve (Figure 2-1). The
speed of the adoption of the innovation is determined by two variables, the speed at which the
adoption takes off, and the speed at which later
growth occurs. Cheap technologies, either in cost
or effort, may have a rapid adoption, while technologies that require a critical mass, such as a tele-

phone, may experience later growth. Ultimately, altering either variable compresses or expands the curve along the x axis.

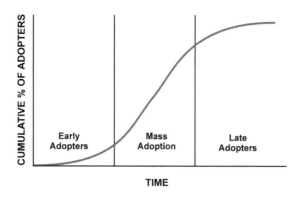

Figure 2-1 Cumulative Number of Cyber Criminals Adopting a Specific Exploit Technology

Not surprisingly, the cumulative number of cyber criminals adopting a technology follows a similar S-curve. If you were looking solely at new adopters taking on a technology at a given point in time, then the graph turns into a bell curve with the maximum growth of adoption in a given time frame at the midsection. Once tool kits arrive to allow the masses to take advantage of an exploit or technique, the adoption rate explodes. Until detection occurs, your losses will continue unchecked. At the point of detection, adoption will then decline and the technology will fall out of favor, assuming your detection makes the adopted tech-

nique less profitable than other techniques
(Figure 2-2).

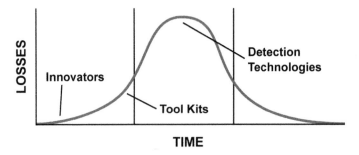

Figure 2-2 Losses Attributed to a Specific Exploit
Technology

If you are unsuccessful in combating the new
technology, then your cumulative losses will grow
exponentially. If you believe some of the numbers
that have been published,[18] then it can be assumed
that roughly 16% to 25% of your user base already
have some form of malware that has been installed
by the cyber criminals. Additionally it is estimated
that approximate 18.59% of all malware contains
some form of key logger or form grabber
technology.[19] With that being said it's possible to
calculate roughly how many accounts are at risk
with the following formula:

18. Panda Security. http://www.pandasecurity.com/infected_or_not/us/.
19. Panda Nanoscan Blog. http://nanoscanblog.pandasecurity.com/
Banker-Trojans-and-online-shopping.aspx (comment posted December 14, 2007).

$$C_{total} \times [1-(1-M_{percent} \times K_{percent})^N] \times A_{Avg}$$

Where:

C_{total} = Total number of clients

$M_{percent}$ = % of computers infected with malware (estimated to be between 16% and 25%)

$K_{percent}$ = % of malware that has keystroke logging capabilities in the wild (estimated at 18.59%)

N = Number of machines the average user logins in from

A_{Avg} = Average number of accounts held by a single client at your firm

Based on the formula above, let us assume that you have 1,000,000 users with 1 account each. Over the life of the account, the average user logs in from only 2 computers. Using the formula above, you see that between 58,603 and 90,790 accounts are already compromised. Restricting the hypothetical users to two computers and limiting users to only one account is extremely conservative and likely understating the potential threat.

Worse yet, your losses will continue until all of these accounts have been hit by the given technology. Fortunately, it is extremely likely that your company will intervene before the cycle reaches its logical conclusion. Losses, however, will approximately follow the S-curve. Assuming that your company can combat the technology in some way but not defeat it with some disruptive countermeasure, the losses from each incident will decline in an inverted S-curve (Figure 2-3).

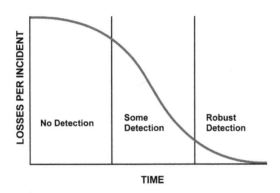

Figure 2-3 Losses per Incident to a Specific Technology

Prior to detection, losses as viewed on an incident basis are at their highest. As you improve, you should be able to decrease the losses quickly. Your ultimate goal is to compress the S-curve along the x axis by deploying an effective countermeasure. Once this occurs your losses should trail off rapidly. If you can locate the perfect countermeasure then the S-curve will become extremely compressed, moving losses specific to that technology rapidly to zero. Losses drop because not only have you effectively stopped the exploit, but you are now impacting the adoption curve by reducing the appeal of the technology to the cyber criminals that are utilizing it, potentially stopping its spread. The biggest difficulty you will face is attempting to figure out where exactly you are on the curve. If you can figure out where a given technology is on the curve, then you should be able to determine if your rate of loss will be accelerating or decelerating. Of course, the hardest part of the exercise is figuring out how to compress your loss curve through technology to minimize the losses.

Understanding Costs

At some point in time you will need to figure out how much to spend to combat your losses. Starting your investigation at a high level is usually the best place to start; at the macro level complex ideas are often clear. At this level you will realize that over time the cost of an incident or series of incidents is sometimes less than the cost of securing against it. As such, it will likely be better for your company to live with the risks and losses, rather than to incur a higher recurring fixed cost and complexity that additional products may introduce.

To put it simply, at the end of the day you will have two costs. The first is a protection cost. This cost is the amount of money you spend in order to provide some level of protection. It may include technology, staff, physical space and other incidental costs to fight fraud. It is important to capture all the components of the protection cost in order to clearly understand the ROI. The second cost is the failure or anticipation cost, which is simply the cost to your company to clean up in the event of a failure. This cost may not only include the estimated value of the lost data, but damage to your image and brand, legal costs, etc. As your protection cost increases, your failure cost should fall. If you sum the failure cost with the protection cost, then you will have the chart below (Figure 2-4). Your optimal spend will be the lowest point of the sum of these two totals.

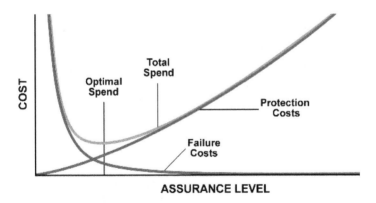

Figure 2-4 Calculating the Optimal Spend

As you can see above on the left side of the chart, in the absence of any money spent on controls, the losses can be infinite. While one can argue that infinite is technically incorrect, losses can be so significant that they shut your company down, so for purposes of this conversation we will leave it as infinite. As you move to the right increasing your assurance level, the rising line is the amount of money you are spending on controls. At some point you are spending more money than a loss would actually cost you however failures are reduced in frequency. So, based on this chart you can graph the sum of the two lines, and your "sweet spot" is quickly revealed. This concept isn't new, insurance companies work on this premise. They collect a fixed fee that they calculate will cover any incident while building in a profit. Unfortunately, in the real world product savings are often hard to quantify, so it is a little harder to locate that sweet spot. However, with a little work you can estimate the failure cost by averaging the estimated maximum possible benefit and estimated minimal possible benefit.

Risk management is an approach that is used by many to manage uncertainty, and client security is filled with uncertainty. It starts with a risk assessment, which assigns a value to your data in the event of a loss, and the probability of an event occurring. This product is then used to develop strategies to manage risk.

Assigning a value to your data in a client security situation is sometimes difficult. In this scenario, quantitative analysis tends to works best. Some easy common sense items would include the cost to fix your client's account after a breach, and the number of people it takes to repair an account. Some of the harder to determine numbers include the damage to your reputation on the micro scale, or better put, what is the probability that the client will no longer do business with you after the event? After 6 months? After a year? If the client does leave you, how much revenue have you lost? How many future customers may you lose because that customer tells others of his experience? How much does it cost to acquire a customer with the same level of assets and the same amount of trading? To get an accurate picture of the value of a customer you will likely need to pull data from multiple sources.

The next step is to assign a frequency to the issue. With client security issues it's more of a question of how often the event will occur, and not the probability of the occurrence. Probability has an upper bound of 1, which means the event will happen, where frequency will act like probability for numbers <1, but it has no upper bounds.

It is usually easiest at this point to work on annual or semi-annual time frames. You will need to calculate the total potential loss of each event. At this point, you are ready to explore solutions, looking at them from a pure cost perspective. The chart below (Figure 2-5) is a very simplified version of what you need, though it may give you a starting point if you are unfamiliar with the process.

		Potential Loss		
		Low	Medium	High
	High	Accept the Risk	Accept the Risk	Your Call
Cost of Protection	Medium	Accept the Risk	Your Call	Eliminate/ Mitigate Risk
	Low	Your Call	Eliminate/ Mitigate Risk	Eliminate/ Mitigate Risk

Figure 2-5. Simplified Risk Management Cheat Sheet

Typically the risks with the greatest loss and the highest frequency of occurrence are given highest priority. While this decision seems easy, you will often run into difficulty when you have events that have high probabilities of occurrence with lower loss and events with low probability of occurrence and high losses. For more information on this subject the author highly recommends Dan Geer's book, *The Economics & Strategies of Data Security*.

Now that you have the basics under your belt it's on to some of the fun stuff.

Terms

2-Tier – An application architecture that separates the user interface from the database.

AES – Advanced Encryption Standard. AES is a symmetric 128-bit block data encryption method with up to a 256 bit encryption key. It was created by the Belgian cryptographers Joan Daemen and Vincent Rijmen. In October 2000, the U.S. government adopted AES as its encryption standard, replacing DES.

Brute Force – A computer problem solving technique that involves enumerating all possible candidates for the solution and then systematically trying each one.

DES – Data Encryption Standard. DES is a symmetric 64-bit block data encryption method with a 56 bit encryption key. It was developed in 1975 and adopted by the U.S. government in 1976.

Key Length – It is the number of bits in an encryption algorithm's key. The key length is sometimes used to measure the relative strength of the encryption algorithm. Longer keys are typically more difficulty to break.

ROI – Return on Investment. ROI is an accounting formula used to obtain the perceived future value of an investment.

CHAPTER 3 # Into the Underground

If you know the enemy and know yourself, your victory will not stand in doubt;

If you know Heaven and know Earth, you may make your victory complete.

- Sun Tzu

Before we dig too deeply into the issues specific to the online brokerage industry, it is important to understand the amount of information available to cyber criminals and the state of the current 'Underground'. The better informed you are about what is actually occurring in the underground, the better prepared you will be to cope with it.

If you are not aware, today the Internet is littered with hundreds of websites and Internet Relay Chat (IRC) rooms dedicated to cyber criminal activities. These rooms once ran on criminal bulletin board systems (BBS), but like everyone else they modernized and moved on to the Internet. Often, when a criminal chat room is taken down by law enforcement or an Internet service provider (ISP), a replacement appears within hours. There are entire IRC networks, not just single servers, dedicated to the underground cyber criminal element. Today there are approximately 40 active servers, all easy for the budding cyber criminal to locate.

In addition to all the IRC channels, there is an endless number of web sites that cater to the cyber criminals. Many of these sites include step-by-step instructions for executing a scam from start to finish. Some of the more popular underground sites over recent years include DarkMarket, Talk-Cash, ScandinavianCarding, CardersMarket, and TheVouched. Most of these web sites have been around for years, with tens of thousands of members. Just because these sites are dealing with illegal and questionable content, the reader should not assume that these are fly-by-night operations. Often these sites are professionally created and offer the cyber criminal a wealth of information and services including: vendor ads with product reviews, point-and-click tool kits to build trojans, bot rental services and phishing scams, how-to guides for everything from credential theft to discreet wire transfers, auction sites for buying and selling anything, and even Q&A sections for new criminals.

A recent Symantec Internet Threat Report[20] shined a light on what private data is available and how much it costs. Credit card number topped the list at 22% of all advertisements, at prices from $0.50 to $5.00 each. Bank accounts followed closely at 21%, with a price range of $30 to $400. Among other interesting items advertised, full identities made up about 6% of advertisements, with a street price of $10 to $150 each, and Social Security numbers came in at 3%, with a price of $5-$7 each.[21]

Most readers of this book would be shocked about the level of detail in some of these underground guides. Cyber criminals list everything

20. Symantec Corporation. "Internet Security Threat Report Volume XII." Symantec Corporation. http://eval.syamantec.com/mktginfo/enterprise/white_papers/entwhitepaper_internent_security_threat_report_xii_09_2007.en?us.pdf (accessed January 19, 2008).
21. Ibid

from what times of day it's easiest to get wires out without fear of a callback from a manager on duty, to unpublished thresholds the various brokers set to flag transactions for further scrutiny. On top of IRC channels and web sites, Instant Messaging (IM) and Peer-to-Peer (P2P) systems are popping up every day to support the flow of information. To make matters worse, many cyber criminals are utilizing encryption to hide their tracks on these systems. Below is a sample of some friendly advice that was posted on one of these questionable servers (Figure 3-1).

```
Precautions
Use Fake IP or Use a VPN while On This Server
Do Not Use Your Real ID in picking up any type
of money
Don't give your real information to anyone
unless you know him/her
keep your self safe on
[name removed].
Thanks!!
```

Figure 3-1

How much information really moves on these servers? The following table illustrates how much information was observed on a single server over a three month period. Below is the number of cards compromised in three months on a single server. As mentioned above, these numbers are from a single server out of at least forty active servers. These totals also don't include all the other communication methods the cyber criminal utilizes.

With these caveats in mind, you may safely assume that the amount of data moved over a three month period is one to two orders of magnitude greater than what is shown below (Figure 3-2).

Amex	210
Visa	87366
MasterCard	35700
Discover	3357

Figure 3-2

As the old adage goes, for the most part there is "honor among thieves". The cyber criminals are typically self-policing, and most systems have dedicated areas to report rippers, those who are known to conduct fraudulent deals. Typically, operators of the network will ban those who have a history of fraud. Most cyber criminals tend to keep records of those that have "ripped" them in the past and are all too happy to share those records with anyone. On the other side of the coin, some sites will bestow the prized "verified" status on well vetted cyber criminals who are considered trustworthy and reliable.

Since most cyber criminals are into a wide variety of fraud, they tend to capitalize on the support structure these sites provide. Below is a quick chat between two criminals (Figure 3-3), one who is looking for a way to move his ill-gotten gains. In this conversation, OS stands for off-shore, and .ee is referencing the webmoney.ee web site.

```
<Criminal 1> whats good os bank
<Criminal 2> u can use webmoney
<Criminal 2> if u can deal with fees its
not OS bank
<Criminal 2> but they wont ever freeze
your account
<Criminal 1> .ee?
<Criminal 2> thats an exchanger
<Criminal 2> www.wmtransfer.com is the
official wm site
```

Figure 3-3

Some cyber criminals market their wares around the clock using automated bots. Below is an example of an advertisement posted by an IRC bot on a popular underground IRC channel (Figure 3-4).

```
<Criminal 3> Sell cvv US ($.90 each), Uk
($1.80 each)Cvv withSSN & DL($10 each)and
ePassporte Account with 7--$ in
ac($40),hacked host($1),Tut Scam CC Full
in VP-ASP Shop($10).shopadmin with 4200
order($175), Tool Calculate Drive Lic-
sence Number($8)... sleeping.  MSG me and
will reply U as soon as I can!
```

Figure 3-4

Ultimately, the goal of most cyber criminals is to extract cash out of what they have stolen. Performing this conversion online is fairly safe for the cyber criminal. Often the biggest challenge to the cyber criminal is where to cash the checks, not bypassing online technologies designed to protect accounts. The second biggest challenge is how to move a large amount of money around. Typically, offshore banking comes into play; several offshore banks will accept such accounts with no questions asked.

Three major forces in the underground make up the bulk of all advertisements:

- ID Thieves – This first group consists of cyber criminals with credentials, account data and personal information from compromised user accounts. This group simply wants to sell the data and move on. Account data is typically sold based on the value of the account or in bulk by the megabyte or gigabyte.
- Drops – This group launders funds and accepts stolen goods.
- Cashiers – This group specializes in physically withdrawing laundered funds out of the compromised account.

Online banking sites have been and remain quite popular targets, with thousands of accounts compromised daily. These compromised accounts may be traded several times before they are actually plundered. Below is an example of some advertisements for services (Figure 3-5).

```
<Criminal 4> have wells and boa logins need
good drop man

<Criminal 5> Have All Bank Infos.  US/Canada/
UK... legit cashiers only msg/me

<Criminal 6> I am Ashley from the State... I got
drops for US banks and need a trus worthy and
understanding man to do deal with... the share is
60/40.. msg me for deal
```

Figure 3-5

Obtaining a fake ID in order to cash out is an easy task in the underground. Many cyber criminals, as you can expect, sell fake IDs or teach others how to create them. The most popular IDs include college IDs, state IDs and drivers' licenses, and an industry has popped up to provide supplies to these cyber criminals.

Cashing out an account is often the most challenging part of an online theft. Most accounts must be cashed out in the country in which the account is physically located. For this task, cyber criminals call upon a cashier. Cashiers, also known as bank brokers, enter the bank, present false ID, and withdraw the contents of the compromised account, no questions asked. They then transfer the funds to the cyber criminal via Western Union, E-gold or Webmoney. For this service, they often demand a 50% take.

This chapter has revealed only a small amount of the goods and services available to the cyber criminal. An entire book could be dedicated to the amount of illegal information available to a cyber criminal.

Terms

BBS – Bulletin Board System. A BBS is computer system that provides functions such as downloading and uploading of software, playing games, reading news and exchanging messages. Typically theses systems were accessed via a dial up modem. As the Internet grew in popularity BBSes slowly faded away.

Byte – A measurement of computer storage. A byte is composed of 8 binary bits. One byte can store one character of data.

e-gold – A company operated by Gold & Silver Reserver, Inc. under e-gold Ltd which allows the instant transfer of precious metal ownership between users.

Gigabyte – A measurement of computer storage. A gigabyte, sometimes referred to as a gig, is 1,073,741,824 bytes.

IM – Instant Messaging. IM provides real-time communication, typically text, to two or more people on a computer network, typically the Internet.

IRC – Internet Relay Chat. IRC is a form of real-time communication similar to instant messaging, however it's typically used for group communication.

The term channel is used to define a single discussion forum. IRC does have the capability for private messaging between two users.

ISP – Internet Service Provider. An ISP is an entity that provides access to the Internet. Most large ISPs have ties to telecommunications or cable companies.

Megabyte – A measurement of computer storage. A megabyte, sometimes referred to as a meg, is 1,048,576 bytes.

P2P – Peer to Peer. P2P is an ad-hoc network that is decentralized, unlike conventional client-server networks.

Webmoney – A company owned by WM Transfer Ltd that allows for online payment.

Western Union – A financial services and communications company that allow for person-to-person money transfers, money orders and other services.

VPN – Virtual Private Network. A VPN is a communications network that tunnels through another network. A typical VPN uses some form of authentication and encryption, though these elements are not necessary.

CHAPTER 4 What Is a Pump-n-Dump?

History teaches that history teaches us nothing

- Georg Wilhelm Friedrich Hegel

There is nothing better than a great Hegel quote to get this chapter moving. This author agrees whole-heartedly with the philosopher. With the speed and mutation of attacks, there is little to gain from looking back five, two, or even one year ago. Historical cases provide only two benefits. First, they give you a complete view of what has been done. Second, they give you an idea of attacker's capabilities and preferences. Once an attack type has peaked it is highly unlikely that it will be recycled with the same success it had at its peak due to the existence of effective countermeasures. That is not to say that recycling won't or doesn't happen, it's just to say that attack strategies and tactics build incrementally on each other. It's unlikely that a very successful future attack would start with anything less than what has been built in the recent past.

We will explore the pump-and-dump scheme and give you a glimpse into the history of a scam that has been around since the start of the stock market. Cyber criminals have computerized this exploit, making pump-and-dump schemes their own. Cyber criminals, like most people, don't reinvent the wheel and they will often modernize a time-tested strategy for the digital age. Much like the mechanization in the world of business, cyber criminals have successfully applied computerization to the pump-and-dump scheme, resulting in greater efficiencies, allowing them greater returns in shorter time frames while reducing their risk.

Most people outside the brokerage industry are unfamiliar with the nature and mechanics of a pump-and-dump scheme. To adequately defend against it, you must understand all of the moving parts of this type of scheme. So what, exactly, is a "pump-and-dump" scheme?

The pump-and-dump, also known as "stock dump" and "hype and dump manipulation", is a term in the financial services for a specific form of financial fraud. A pump-and-dump usually involves artificially inflating or depressing the price of a security through untrue or exaggerated promotion. This scheme is one of the most common forms of securities fraud on the Internet today.

Readers may be familiar with the 1987 movie Wall Street, staring Michael Douglas and Charlie Sheen, which involved a pump-and-dump scheme towards the end of the movie. In the movie, the main character, Bud Fox manipulates the stock price of the fictitious company Blue Star in order to keep Gordon Gekko from liquidating it.

Just like the movie, the goal of the dumper is to shift the demand of the security in a direction financially beneficial to the dumper. In most situations, it means selling a security that the dumper previously purchased cheaply, at an inflated price. When the promotion of the security stops, or the promotion is exposed as being untrue, the artificial demand is removed, causing a collapse in the price of the investment, leaving many investors holding the bag. The collapse can damage the security so severely that the market price of the security after the pump-and-dump is actually lower than where it started. Often the price of the affected security remains depressed for days, weeks or even months after the event. Typically, this depression is due to a large number of investors holding on to the security in hopes that it will return to a price where they can make a profit. As a result, the security can become even more illiquid. The price of the security may even remain depressed for years due to investors refusing to invest in the stock of a company that has been manipulated in the past, even if the company had no involvement. It is important to note, that in the stock market, it is possible for the dumper to make money no matter which direction the stock is moving. Since the dumper is in control of the price movement, there is little risk to him. The dumper can take the other side of the trade and short sell a security and then push the price down in order to profit. The current trend is for the dumper to go long on a security and if the security can be short sold, short it towards the top. This type of double dipping is likely to leave a trail of bread crumbs right to the dumper. This combination of actions indicates either a very inexperienced cyber criminal unaware of the potential consequences, or a very skilled one that knows he has sufficiently covered his tracks.

The pump-and-dump scam works best with securities that trade at low volumes where it is easier to upset the price with small increases in volume. Typically manipulation will start with Over-The-Counter Bulletin Board (OTCBB) and Pink Sheet securities. If you are successful in identifying fraud occurring in one of these symbols, then you will notice that the cyber criminals tactics will change and they will move to thinly traded listed stocks, or possibly into options. Cyber criminals tend to mine an attack vector until it becomes unprofitable.

In the United States, as in many countries, the pump-and-dump scheme is illegal as it reduces confidence in the market. Despite the illegality, however, pump-and-dumps remain very common. While it would seem that this type of activity is easily policed, it isn't. The problem is that often the dumper keeps a low profile and often makes less than $10,000 dollars in profit. This profit may seem like a large amount of money, but in the world of finance, it is the proverbial needle in the haystack. Legitimate investors will often have "good until canceled" orders in place. These orders are orders that are placed days or weeks in advance to sell out of a security when it reaches a certain price. Investors may also have standing orders with their brokers to get them out of these securities. The result is that there may be hundreds, even thousands, of investors and day traders that profited during the pump-and-dump that may need to be investigated to attempt to identify the dumper.

The 21st century has updated the classic pump-and-dump scheme using new technology and methods. While fraudsters in the past relied on cold calls, the emergence of the Internet offers a cheaper and easier way of reaching large numbers of potential investors. Over the past few years there have been several iterations of the classic pump-and-dump scheme, each building on the prior one and becoming more sophisticated. The first iteration of this scheme simply replaced stock touting over the phone or via mail with a cheaper, faster method: the Internet, e-mail, and phony websites. Much more importantly, this type of attack evolved by removing the need for a person to be duped into purchasing a security. Cyber criminals correctly surmised that it was more efficient to just remove the investor and trade on his behalf, utilizing stolen credentials.

Spam, spam, spam

Cyber criminals tend to take advantage of as many avenues of exploitation as they have available to them. It should be of no surprise that unsolicited bulk email (UBE), also known as "spam", is one of the most frequently used methods. Spamming, as it relates to pump-and-dump, can occur via newsgroups, blogs and other methods and need not rely on delivery of an email. In some cases it may even utilize physical mail. Currently, there are two main types of pump-and-dump spam on the Internet. Both of these types of spam attacks were growing by leaps and bounds until the Federal Trade Commission (FTC) and the Securities and Exchange (SEC) recently turned their attention to any spam that touted the purchase of a stock.

The first type of spamming attack is known as the "basic spam" attack and it is carried out completely by a single individual or group. In this type of attack, the individual or group is responsible for all aspects, from selecting a security, to composing the spam message, to the mass mailing of that message. Typically, these basic spam attacks are less professional than a sponsored spam attack (see below). They are also less targeted and often picked up by spam filters at a higher rate. That's not to say there aren't exceptions to the rule.

Jonathan Lebed was one of the earlier adopters of using e-mails and web site posts, but he wasn't the last. In late 2000, the Securities and Exchange Commission (SEC) settled a case against Mr. Lebed, who was at the time a fifteen year old high school student. At the time, he was the youngest person ever prosecuted by the SEC for stock fraud. According to the case, between September 1999 and February 2000, Mr. Lebed used his E-Trade account to make multiple purchases of thinly traded securities, those trading less than one hundred thousand shares a day. After purchasing a given security, he would go to financially-oriented message boards and post hundreds of promotional messages under fictitious names. On days Mr.

Lebed posted to the news groups, the securities he touted would shoot up. Volumes would often jump over a million shares a day. According to the file, his smallest one-day gain was approximately twelve thousand dollars. His biggest one-day gain was approximately seventy four thousand dollars. The settlement ended with Mr. Lebed agreeing to hand over his illicit gains, plus interest, which came to two hundred and eighty-five thousand dollars; in addition he admitted no wrong doing. What most people don't know is that the case only included eleven of his transactions. In actuality, he had managed to make over eight hundred thousand dollars, pocketing close to half a million dollars after settling with the SEC. Call that a first mover advantage!

The Lebed case simply involved touting a stock. This approach was very similar to the old pump-and-dump schemes, but instead of involving a phone or fliers, this incident used a new tool for the time, namely the Internet. This example shows that even back in 2000, the Internet was already a key tool for investors to move information around at high speed. It also shows that those with a little know how could take advantage of the Internet to make a great deal of money.

The second type of spamming attack is known as "sponsored spam". The sponsored spam attack involves two independent people or groups. The sponsor is the person or group responsible for selecting the target security to pump. The sponsor may or may not help with the design of the pump email message. The second individual or group is the career spammer, and is responsible for developing the pump email message along with the targeting and distribution of the spam.

A sponsored spam attack starts with a sponsor searching for a career spammer with a large, active bot net. A bot net is a collection of compromised computers running autonomous programs under the control of a common command and control structure. The owner of the bot net is typically referred to as a bot herder. The bot net may be either owned by the spammer or rented. Once these two have located each other and a deal is struck, the spammer then starts spamming a large number of victims over the course of several days. An average career spammer has control of approximately 70,000 bots and is capable of sending out in excess of 100 million emails per day. At this point it's likely you may be in denial over the 70,000 bots number, so I'll back that number up with numbers from the researchers.

It is estimated that there are approximately 600 to 800 million computers connected to the Internet today. Of those computers, approximately 100 million to 150 million computers are already part of a bot network.[22] Vint Cerf, sometimes called the

---

22. Weber, Tim. "Criminals 'may overwhelm the web'." BBC News. http://news.bbc.co.uk/2/hi/business/6298641.stm (accessed December 22, 2007).

father of the Internet, has echoed that number and stated that there are 100 to 150 million compromised machines in play. Trend Micro states a more conservative number, of 70 million existing compromised machines, and 8 to 9 million new compromised machines becoming active each month. In an interview with Red Herring, Merrick Furst noted the rapid rise in bot armies, and suggested that about 80 percent of spam is created by bot nets. He went on to say that more than 250,000 new machines are conscripted each day, falling in line with Trend Micro's number.[23] Symantec, more conservatively, has stated that over 10,000 recruited machines become active each day.

The activity of these bot networks is just as staggering. In 2006, security firm Damballa was tracking approximately 333,000 unique instances of bots carrying out nefarious commands. One year later they were tracking over 7.3 million unique instances. Rick Wesson, CEO of Support Intelligence has stated that on a typical day over 40% of the computers on the Internet are being used for nefarious purposes.

What's worse is the current market rate for bot rental. At the time of this writing, the cost for renting a single bot is approximately $0.04[24] to $0.13

---

23. Red Herring. "Q&A: Bot?Buster Merrick Furst." Red Herring. http://www.redherring.com/Article.aspx?a=15459&hed=Q%26amp%3bA%3a+Bot?Buster+Merrick+Furst (accessed September 13, 2007).

per day[25] depending on the source you quote. You can also get deep discounts for longer term rentals at a mere $1 per bot per month. At these rates, just about anyone can afford to rent a large number of bots.

Once the spamming operation starts, the sponsor will sell his stock anywhere from several hours to a full day after spamming. Based on anecdotal evidence, the sponsor typically makes 6% - 12% profit. The career spammer is typically paid based on how much he was able to raise the price of the stock.

The sponsored spamming attack is much more difficult to trace back to the criminals responsible. Spammers are hired to pump a stock on behalf of an investor and there is often little, if any, evidence to connect the two together. Knowledgeable career spammers are extremely cautious. In spammer forums, the spammer often warns the sponsor that no records of the transaction should exist. The two parties will never communicate via email or telephone. Spammers strongly advise against writing anything down. It's clear the spammers are aware that what they are doing is completely illegal and they could face stiff penalties if caught. If law enforcement manages to beat the odds and track

24. Team Cymru, "the underground economy: priceless," Login, vol. 31, no. 6, pp. 7-16, Dec. 2006.
25. Warren, Peter. "Hunt for Russia's web criminals." GardianUnlimited. http://www.guardian.co.uk/technology/2007/nov/15/news.crime (accessed December 8, 2007).

down the spammer, it is highly unlikely that that the spammer will be able to identify the sponsor. Deniability has become a consistent component of such fraud.

How big are the current sponsored spam attacks? In June of 2007, a very large sponsored spam attack touting a German company, OYQ.F, flooded the Internet with approximately five billion messages, causing the trading volume of the stock to increase 1,300%, and the stock price to jump significantly over a span of two days. The five billion messages represented approximately 8% of all spam messages sent on the Internet that day, according to experts.[26] The German spam message utilized a new technique. Until this point, spammers had been typically using image based spam to bypass filters. This time the spammers used a PDF file attached to what appeared to be a legitimate investment newsletter. This new approach allowed the message to not only bypass most spam filters, but the professional look of the attachment was convincing enough to dupe more people into purchasing the security.

Tools & Tips: An excellent resource to locate stocks touted via spam is Spamnation. This web site allows you to examine a daily list of securities

---

26. Weiss, Todd R. "Massive stock spam uses crafty PDF to lure investors." Computerworld (June 21, 2007), http://www.computerworld.com/action/article.do?command=printArticleBasic&articleId=9025425.

that trade on various exchanges, including overseas. While the list isn't comprehensive, it is still an excellent resource. Spamnation can be found at: http://www.spamnation.info/stocks/

As of the writing of this book, spammers have moved on to MP3 files, also known as "audio spam," to tout their stocks. MIME tricks are also becoming more prevalent to slip past anti-spam systems.[27] It's likely that even these techniques will further evolve. Only time will tell who will be victorious. It is likely no one will win this arms race as there is a great amount of incentive for both sides to win.

The Phony Web Site

One of the earliest examples of a phony website scam appeared in April, 1994. A former employee of PairGain Technologies posted a fraudulent message on an Internet website that looked similar to a popular news service called Bloomberg. The message stated that a major competitor was in the process of acquiring PairGain, then trading around $8.50, for $19 per share. The fake site was so convincing that it convinced even experienced money managers on Wall Street and news services, such

27. Virus Bulletin. "MIME tricks beat email virus scanners." Virus Bulletin. http://www.virusbtn.com/news/2006/12_11a_virus.xml (accessed January 2, 2008).

as thestreet.com, that the news was true. The end
result was an unprecedented flurry of trading,
which caused the company's stock to rise from
$8.50 a share to over $11.25 a share, a more than a
30% increase. Even after the message and website
were debunked, PairGain's stock remained elevated, eventually closing up over 10% from its
prior close, a net gain of over $46.5 million dollars.
Charges were later pressed against the former
employee, though others got to keep their gains.

A more recent example involved Emulex in
August, 2000. In this case a web-based news service, Internet Wire, posted a phony press release
just as the markets opened. The fraud was
launched by a 23 year old college student, Mark
Jakob, a former Internet Wire employee who
recently lost money selling Emulex. Jakob sold the
stock short prior to submitting the phony press
release. The press release stated that the Emulex
CEO had just resigned and they had been forced to
restate 1998 and 1999 earnings as losses instead of
gains. Other respected news services, including
Bloomberg and CBS Marketwatch, jumped on the
news story within half an hour. Emulex's stock
opened around $110 dollars a share, but quickly
dropped down to $43 dollars a share before NAS-
DAQ stepped in and halted trading in the stock.
This fake news item resulted in a net loss of over $2
billion dollars in market capitalization. Jakob realized a profit of over $54,000 dollars as the stock fell
and then continued to sell shares short as the stock
declined. His total profit after the scheme was

complete was over $241,000 dollars. In December of 2000, Jakob pleaded guilty to two counts of securities fraud and one count of wire fraud. A federal judge, in the SEC's civil action, entered an injunction against Jakob prohibiting him from violating the antifraud provisions of the federal securities laws in the future. The court ordered Jakob to repay all of his gains and losses avoided from his scheme, plus interest, in an amount of approximately $353,000. The judge also ordered a civil penalty of $102,642. Emulex fortunately recovered from this hoax relatively unscathed.

Enter the Trojan Horse

In 2003, a Pennsylvania teenager marked the beginning of a more complex generation of pump-and-dump scams. Just nineteen years old at the time, Van Dinh was one of the first known cyber criminals to use a trojan horse to co-opt another user's online brokerage account. This scam at the time seemed to be a one-time event, but as it turns out, it was just a small glimpse at the epidemic to come.

Dinh has the dubious distinction of being the first person charged by the Securities and Exchange Commission with a fraud involving both computer hacking and identity theft. In July of 2003, Mr. Dinh was the owner of approximately $90,000 in put options. These options could have delivered a large payoff to Mr. Dinh if Cisco Sys-

tems Inc. stock dropped below $15.00 a share.
Unfortunately for Mr. Dinh, at the time Cisco stock
was not about to go below the fifteen dollar strike
price, making the options likely to expire worthless. Rather than take the loss, Mr. Dinh allegedly
constructed a plan to offload the contracts on an
innocent investor. Mr. Dinh built a list of targets
by posting innocuous queries as "Stanley Hirsch"
to a public forum on the trading discussion site
stockcharts.com. Dinh then noted the e-mail
addresses of those who responded. The next day,
using the alias "Tony T. Riechert," he spammed
those addresses with an offer to participate in a
beta test of a new stock charting tool.

The "stock charting" tool turned out to be a trojan horse called the "Beast", according to the SEC.
An unsuspecting investor, unnamed in the complaints, ran the program, and sometime thereafter
accessed his online brokerage account with TD
Waterhouse. Operating silently in the background,
the Beast logged every keystroke. Mr. Dinh allegedly signed in later and downloaded the logs,
obtaining the man's username and password to his
TD Waterhouse account.

A few days later, Mr. Dinh put his Cisco
options up for sale at an inflated price through his
own online broker, and used the stolen ID and
password to place a series of matching buy orders
through the victim's account, "depleting almost all
of the account's available cash," according to the
SEC. The account held approximately $47,000 at

the time. With the account drained, Mr. Dinh still held some remaining Cisco contracts, which expired, worthless, on July 19th. Mr. Dinh's scheme managed to shave his losses by approximately $37,000 after the broker's commission, according to the SEC report.

"Despite the use of complex anonymizer programs and other cloaking devices, our staff was able to unravel this conduct quickly," said Linda Chatman Thomsen, Deputy Director of the SEC's Enforcement Division, in a statement. "To those who attempt to use the perceived anonymity of the Internet to victimize investors, our message remains clear: we will track you down and hold you accountable." A federal criminal complaint was filed in Massachusetts against Mr. Dinh for computer intrusion, in addition to wire, mail and securities fraud in connection with the alleged scheme. Dinh was eventually sentenced on May 5, 2004 to 13 months of imprisonment, to be followed by three years of supervised release. Additionally, $3800 in fines were imposed. Prior to his sentencing, Dinh paid full restitution to the victim investor in the amount of $46,986, which represented the entire amount of money taken from the investor's account.

Who is Running Pump and Dump Scams Today?

It is a good idea to know who your enemy is. With such knowledge you can effectively combat your enemy. So just who are the people running these scams? They are a broad cross-section of the computer underground, from basic criminals playing with pre-made point-and-click kits, to foreign organized crime syndicates that have discovered a new lucrative revenue stream.

The Script Kiddie

Script kiddies, as their name implies, are the same kids that crack software so they can win at games. They often use the work of others in the form of tool kits or sample code. Typically, their motivation is to make a few dollars to buy a new computer or finance their online gaming fees. The script kiddie is generally unsophisticated, and while they know enough to execute an attack, they do not understand the subtle intricacies of a specific attack. This naiveté often leads this group into making numerous mistakes, such as reusing the same IP address, or not rotating their user agent in their browser. These beginner mistakes not only let you detect and stop them, but often you can follow the trail right back to them. When you are looking to eliminate the low hanging fruit, these are the first guys you will be trimming from the tree.

This group essentially invented phishing, an attack we will learn more about later in this book. As it turns out, that type of behavior is quite unusual for this group, as script kiddies typically run canned attacks rather than invent new attack vectors. Even though this group is itself unsophisticated, it has access to increasingly sophisticated tools and tool kits. While it's possible to easily locate script kiddies today, this task may not be so easy in the future.

The Cracker

Crackers are the most dangerous enemy your firm must face. Crackers are typically very sophisticated and knowledgeable programmers that can develop their own code, compromise even some secured computers, and in general cause havoc on a large scale. This group is researching and developing new attacks. Crackers are also the people developing phishing kits, worms, trojans and the point-and-click tool kits often utilized by script kiddies.

Some crackers may also have their own bot nets. These bots will send spam, perform denial of service attacks (DoS), act as web servers, or anything else the cracker wishes. It should be noted that at this level of sophistication, a cracker likely specializes in a specific attack or software type. For example, one cracker may specialize in software to distribute malware, while another cracker may specialize in the malware itself, while yet another may specialize in phishing.

Organized Crime

Organized crime appears to just be getting its feet wet in the online world. Until recently large attacks were often executed by organized criminals, but not organized crime. Organized crime brings to the table the ability to provide large amounts of working capital, an existing infrastructure to launder money, an ability to focus a large number of cyber criminals on one goal, and to provide protection. As organized crime gets more and more involved, one can believe that attacks will get more specific, more complex, and larger in scale. With working capital, it is possible to hire programming talent away from legitimate work. For example, in Russia the average programmer makes less than $10,000 a year.[28] Imagine the doors that open when an organization can spend tens of millions of dollars up front to double or triple that investment down the line.

Terrorists

Though there are currently no direct reports of terrorists being involved in cyber crime; it's safe to assume that they are. In 2002, the Federal Bureau of Investigation stated in Congressional testimony

28. Payscale, Inc. http://www.payscale.com.

that "The impact is greater than just the loss of money... Terrorists and terrorist groups require funding to perpetrate their terrorist agendas... Identity theft is a key catalyst for fueling many of these methods".[29]

The Insider

Unfortunately, good apples sometimes go bad. Typically, the insider has a low paying job and is looking to make some money on the side. Most often the insider is working with one of the groups above. The transaction is typically a list of user ids & passwords, the email addresses' of your customers, or some other confidential information. An insider with a little knowledge can go undetected for long periods of time. Fortunately, with the use of some modern data leak prevention tools, such as Digital Guardian from Verdasys,[30] you can greatly reduce this attack vector.

29. U.S. Congress. The Identity Theft Penalty Enhancement Act: Hearing on S. 2541, 2002.

30. Verdasys. http://www.verdasys.com.

Terms

Anonymizer – An intermediary device or
devices designed to hide the IP address
of a system.

Blog – An online diary or journal that is frequently updated, often daily. The word
blog is derived from the term web log.

Bot – A computer compromised by malware
that allows an attacker to control it. The
bot is controlled via a remote command
and control structure. Typically a bot is
used for denial of service attacks, malware distribution, and for sending spam.

Bot Herder – The owner and operator of a bot
net.

Bot Nets – A collection of compromised
machines under the control of a common
command and control structure.

Cracker – Criminal hackers also known as black
hats. These users are very skilled programmers with specialized skill sets,
such as malware, phishing, or root kits.

DoS – Denial of Service, an attempt to make a
computer resource unavailable. Typically a DoS attack involves overwhelm-

ing the target with traffic so that it cannot respond to legitimate requests.

FTC – The Federal Trade Commission, it is an independent agency of the US government whose principal mission is the promotion of consumer protection.

IP Address – Internet Protocol Address, a unique address that allows devices on a network to locate and communicate with each other. An IP Address is often dynamic and as such it cannot be relied upon as a unique identifier.

Malware – A generic term for any software intentionally designed to cause harmful effects to a system or data.

MIME – Multipurpose Internet Mail Extensions. MIME is an Internet standard that extends the format of email to support non-ASCII character sets, non-text attachments, multi-part message bodies, and non-ascii header information.

NASDAQ – The National Association of Securities Dealers Automated Quotient. NASDAQ was the world's first electronic stock market.

OCR – Optical Character Recognition. OCR is a piece of computer software designed to translate written data into machine readable text.

OTCBB – Over the Counter Bulletin Board. OTCBB is an electronic quote system that provides real-time data on many over the counter securities that aren't listed on a national securities exchange. Companies quoted on the system must be current with all required SEC filings. There are no requirements for market capitalization, minimum share price, corporate governance or other requirements to be listed. Companies without SEC filings may be quoted in the Pink Sheets, and most companies quoted on the OTCBB are also quoted in the Pink Sheets.

Phishing – A method designed to steal personal information directly over the Internet through impersonation of the sender and content.

Pink Sheets – An electronic quote system that provides data on over the counter securities. The name comes from the pink paper the quotes were printed on before the system went electronic. Since there are no requirements to be listed on the Pink Sheets, these securities tend to be extremely risky.

Put Option – Also known as a "put", it is an option contract that gives the holder the right to sell a set number of shares of a security to the writer of the option at a specified strike price up to a specified expiration date. The seller must pur-chase the underlying asset at the strike price if the buyer exercises the option.

Script Kiddie – Cyber criminals that used canned scripts and programs developed by others to accomplish their goals. Typically the script kiddie does not understand the script or code he is using or the damage it can cause. Crackers use this description as a derogatory term.

Trojan – A malicious software program that appears to be a legitimate piece of soft-ware in order to trick an unsuspecting user into executing the software and infecting his computer. The term trojan horse, or trojan for short, comes from the mythical tactic used by the Greeks between 1500 and 1200 BC.

UBE – Unsolicited Bulk E-Mail. UBE, more commonly known as spam, involves sending large numbers of similar email messages to large numbers of recipients.

Virus – A malicious computer program that copies itself in order to infect a computer. A virus can only be spread when its host is moved to an uninfected computer. Typically, a virus spreads via floppy disks, CDs, USB drives or email. Unlike a worm, a virus cannot propagate itself without some user interaction.

Worm – A self-replicating, malicious computer program. A worm, unlike a virus, is self contained and sends copies of itself to other computers without user intervention.

CHAPTER 5 The Dumper's Account

Isne tibi melius suadet, qui 'rem facias, rem, si possis, recte, si non, quocumque modo rem

Rough Translation: Make money, money by any fair means if you can, if not, by any means

- Horace

Now that you have an overview of the history of stock manipulation, we will explore each phase of a pump-and-dump and speculate as to how these attacks may morph in the future. In this chapter, we will examine the account of the person who ultimately profits from the scheme. There are some subtle tell-tale signs that may allow a broker early detection of these accounts. With some fore-warning you can mitigate the worst of the losses that you and your fellow firms may experience.

The first step of the pump-and-dump scam is for the dumper, the person who will ultimately profit, to open several accounts at one or more brokerages. Because the dumper is engaging in illegal activities, the experienced dumper almost always provides false personal information. The goal of the dumper is to leave no trace of his actual identity, a goal that isn't always as straightforward as it seems. Unlike crackers, script kiddies will often open the dump account under their own names since they lack the capability to move money titled under other names. Professionals will often just steal the identity of someone else to minimize their exposure.

When the dumper uses stolen identities; the dumper may only use a partial set of personally identifiable information (PII). The reason is simple; the cyber criminal knows full well that when a new account is opened, the financial services company immediately sends information out to a new account holder. If a criminal uses a stolen identity with a set of perfectly matched data, it is more than likely that the victim would be tipped off by a welcome packet before the cyber criminal can execute his plan.

In most cases, the dumper's account uses a stolen identity with a valid full name and valid social security number. The dumper then provides a non-existent address, phone number or other fake identifying information on the signup form. Invalid account information is a huge red flag for any financial services firm; it's often the only chance your firm has to detect the cyber criminal before he executes his plan.

Tools & Tips: Simply checking an applicant's phone number and address against what is listed in the phone book may help you zero in on fraudulent accounts. The proliferation of cell phones may hamper this effort but it may be worth looking into. Additionally, sharing lists of bad social security numbers, addresses and other fake information with your peers may help all of you to detect future fraud.

Another typical mistake made by most cyber criminals, even the professionals, is the recycling of certain information. The most commonly recycled data points are email addresses, street names and phone numbers. Some systems, such as Mantas' Anti-Money Laundering systems, may be able to detect basic relations between accounts. No present system is evolved enough, however, to search for subtle similarities.

Tools & Tips: Carefully check any "Return to Sender" mail to a new client. Validate these clients' identities with the email address on record at credit service companies such as Equifax, TransUnion or Experian. This method will allow a company to quickly reduce a portion of their fraud. Be aware, however, that if the dumper is fast enough he can, in fact, use a completely stolen identity including the actual mailing address.
A more sophisticated method for an antifraud system would be to use an outside service that requires correct answers to knowledge based questions only the owner of the identity would know to open an account. EMC's VerId is one such service, where a new applicant may be asked questions like "What was the make and model of the car you bought in 1995?"
As of this writing there are a handful of cyber criminals that are capable of passing VerId.[31] While not foolproof, these systems add additional controls to deter cyber criminals. The key is to remember that the more layers of security your company deploys, the more likely a criminal will make a mistake and be detected.

As you may have guessed, experienced dumpers stick to smaller financial service companies that cannot afford sophisticated monitoring tools.

---

31. RSA, RSA Identity Verification, VerId Product Brochure, 2008.

More specifically they prefer financial service companies that have the easiest methods to move large amounts of cash quickly. Firms offering fast ACH and wires or debit card access are often targeted.

You may be wondering where all this personal information comes from. It comes from multiple sources. Hackers break into small databases and aggregate the results. Over time, they can build complete financial histories from a mixture of stolen data and Internet searches. Security researcher David Litchfield estimates that there are nearly 500,000 databases exposed on the Internet without a firewall.[32] When you add in the number of databases that are secured by at least a firewall, but fail to change generic passwords or patch security flaws, the count becomes more than the opponent can use. The US government, from the Census Bureau[33] to defense contractors,[34] happens to be a large source of personal information that the cyber criminals use for committing identity theft. Even the SEC has exposed the social security numbers of some top executives.[35]

---

32. McMillan, Robert. "Half a million database servers 'have no firewall'." ComputerWorldUK (November, 2007), http://www.computerworlduk.com/management/security/data?control/news/index.cfm?newsid=6198.

33. Nakashima, Ellen. "U.S. Exposes Personal Data." Washington Post, April 21, 2007.

34. NetworkWorld. "Data breach exposed 900,000 soldier, government employee health records." NetworkWorld (July, 2007), http://www.networkworld.com/community/node/17717.

Now that the dumper has chosen an identity to use for his brokerage account, the dumper must cover his Internet protocol (IP) address tracks. Once the pump-and-dump scheme is executed, the wheels of justice start turning, law enforcement begins tracking back the initial IP address. It is just a matter of time before it is tracked back to either a dead-end or to its source. The dumper must hide his IP address or he will quickly find his door being kicked down.

Tools & Tips: A possible anti-fraud system would be to match up the state or country listed on the application to the IP address registered on your online signup form. If the location of the IP address isn't close to the address on the form it may be a clue that the application is fraudulent. Corporate networks, however, can trigger a number of false positives. Often corporations route all their internal traffic destined for the Internet out through a single IP at a single location known as NAT, creating a location discrepancy. You can reduce these false positives by comparing the owner of the IP address space to the place of employment listed on the new account application form. Long term, a trustworthy geo-coding of the Internet would yield significant value.

Although this system may report a few false

---

35. Harrison, Ann. "SEC database exposes Social Security Numbers." CNN. http://www.cnn.com/TECH/computing/9903/29/secssn.idg/ (accessed September 18, 2007).

positives, it should be possible to manually review the "kick-outs". Additionally, these kick-outs may be candidates for additional screening in the form of a credit check, further address validation, or at least a phone call. Again, with a stolen identity, it is within the cyber criminal's capability to do his homework and match answers perfectly. However, even when the criminal uses 100% correct information, he has to work quickly, resulting in a greater chance of error and exposure.

While pump-and-dump attacks before the end of 2006 commonly used the same IP address for a given group of attacks, the current trend has shifted to rotating IP addresses. The use of anonymous proxies and the TOR network has increased rapidly, and is practically main stream. Even now, however, these resources are being replaced with compromised machines (BOTs) that the cyber criminals have acquired. In addition, recent intelligence has revealed the existence of HaxTOR, a TOR type network built specifically by and for cyber criminals. The HaxTOR network is roughly 4,000 nodes strong, however cyber criminals have been seen rotating the IP addresses of these nodes sometimes up to 20 times a day. It is not unusual to see over 100,000 unique IP addresses assigned to these nodes in a given month, making it nearly impossible to use any form of black listing. The current HaxTOR network is already larger than the original TOR network and is expected to continue to grow. To make matters worse, you can take down 95%+ of the network and it will still continue to function.

Tools & Tips: While IP Addresses have some use, an alternative offensive weapon would be to attempt to fingerprint the computer itself. Typically, cyber criminals aren't rotating every unique piece of information about their computers, so good candidates would be the media access control (MAC) address, the Windows product key, or other unique values that either don't change or are unlikely to change. Duplicates of these fingerprints in your online signup forms may be a red flag.

The Onion Routing (TOR/HaxTOR) Primer

For readers not familiar with onion routing, here is a brief description on how it works. Onion routing is a technique for anonymous communication over a network developed by David Goldschlag, Michael Reed, and Paul Syverson.[36] It is based on David Chaum's mix network;[37] but includes additional features, such as the concept of "routing onions". These "onions" encode routing information in a set of encrypted layers. The goal

---

36. Goldschlag, David, Reed, Michael, and Syverson, Paul, "Onion Routing," Communications of the ACM, vol. 42, iss. 2, pp. 39-41, Feb. 1999.

37. Chaum, David, "Untraceable Electronic Mail, Return Addresses, and Digital Pseudonyms," Communications of the ACM, vol. 24, no. 2, pp. 84-90, Feb. 1981.

---

of onion routing is to protect the privacy of both the sender and recipient of a message, while also providing protection for message content as it moves across the network. Traffic travels from source to destination via a sequence of proxies, called onion routers, which re-route messages in an unpredictable path. To prevent an adversary from eavesdropping on message content, messages are encrypted between routers. The advantage of onion routing is that it is not necessary to trust each cooperating router; if one or more routers are compromised, anonymous communication can still be achieved. This security exists because each router in an onion router network accepts messages, re-encrypts them, and transmits to another onion router. An attacker with the ability to monitor every onion router in a network might be able to trace the path of a message through the network, but an attacker with more limited capabilities will have greater difficulty even if he or she controls one or more onion routers on the message's path.

Onion routing does not provide perfect sender or receiver anonymity against all possible eavesdroppers. Correlation can determine who is sending what, however the eavesdropper would need to observe both the entrance and exit nodes of the conversation. Currently, it is believed that only the National Security Agency (NSA) has this capability.

The most popular onion routing system as of this writing is TOR (the onion router), a second-generation onion router proposed at the 13th USENIX Security Symposium by Roger Dingledine, Nick Mathewson, and Paul Syverson.[38] Currently there are approximately 1000 active TOR nodes available on the Internet at any given time.

Additional work is taking place to reduce the privacy of TOR by observing only a segment of the network. Currently the use of TOR provides for a strong degree of unlinkability, the notion that an eavesdropper cannot easily determine both the sender and receiver of a given message. Even within these confines, onion routing does not provide any absolute guarantee of privacy; rather, it provides a continuum in which the degree of privacy is generally a function of the number of participating routers versus the number of compromised or malicious routers. While TOR's privacy can be compromised by adding a small set of malicious routers, the cyber criminal's version, HaxTOR, would need a significantly larger number of malicious routers to snoop on data, and thereby allow legal agencies the ability to track back data to its source.

Tools & Tips: Watch logins that originate from proxy servers, satellite service providers or

---

38. Dingledine, Roger, Mathewson, Nick, and Syverson, Paul, "Tor: The Second?Generation Onion Router," Usenix Security 2004, Aug. 2004.

TOR nodes for suspicious activity. Several vendors will sell you proxy and satellite IP address lists and often a lot of geolocation databases, such as those by vendors like MaxMind, contain lists of proxy servers and satellite service providers in them. TOR databases are freely available on the Internet and should also be screened.

Automation Primer

It is important to note that a cyber criminal may register a large number of accounts at once in order to spread money around, or to prevent his account from being locked, freezing his funds. With this being said, the cyber criminal may attempt to script his account openings, and then fund only a subset of accounts. The cyber criminal's logic is that a large number of accounts being opened on the same day may overwhelm a broker and force them to not thoroughly check all applications or to examine only a sampling of new account forms. In the past, the best way to defeat automated signup systems was to use CAPTCHA. As we will see in the countermeasures chapter, even CAPTCHA can be beaten by cyber criminals using a variety of creative methods.

Tools & Tips: If you do implement CAPTCHA, it's important to put a time limit on solving the CAPTCHA, putting pressure on the attacker. You should also be aware that there are client

experience issues around CAPTCHA. CAPT-
CHA, both text and picture based, is hard to
read by the visually impaired, and it is impossible to use for blind visitors and automated systems.

Funding the Account

While the funding and staging of the drop
account seems like an easy step, the cyber criminal
does need to do some homework to properly execute this section of the plan. Extra effort by the
cyber criminal in this step makes it less likely to be
detected, allowing for a safer getaway. A misstep
in this phase can cause not only the loss of capital,
but potentially leave a trail of bread crumbs
directly back to the cyber criminal. The cyber
criminal has to make sure he covers his tracks as
well as he did with the setup of the account. In
addition, he must now move funds without causing suspicion. Transferring funds is one of the biggest pitfalls, as money movement is closely
watched and audited due to numerous industry
regulations.

The cyber criminal has two major ways to fund
the brokerage account. He can use his own cash or
he can use a stolen bank account. No matter which
method the cyber criminal uses, it is extremely
likely that the criminal will utilize one or more
intermediaries to obscure the trail of the funds.
Currently, digital gold currency providers are used

at some point in the transaction because they are not legally required to perform the various background checks that a bank would do for a new account. Another reason digital gold currency is favored is that most currency transactions are non-reversible, even in the case of legitimate errors or unauthorized expenditures.

Not all e-gold exchange providers are equally questionable. GoldNow, for example, requires a higher level of identification upon account setup than most banks.

If the funds are stolen, the cyber criminal will likely move funds to a drop or through a digital gold provider first. By the time any trail can be established, the funds will have been used for trading. A drop is a person that specializes in dealing with 'virtual money' and with some ability to launder the money. Drops are usually located in countries with very lax e-crime laws, like Bolivia, Indonesia and Malaysia. The drops represent safe, legitimate bank accounts for money to be transferred into illegally, and paid out of legitimately.

Once the cyber criminal has determined his funding method, only a few steps remain to getting money into the account. While the current intermediary of choice is e-gold, they are certainly not the only player in town. Often, e-gold accounts are not allowed as a funding method so there would be one additional intermediary, further increasing anonymity. That intermediary would typically move stolen funds to a preloaded credit or debit card. Preloaded credit/debit cards are both new and numerous, and allow easy loading of cash via Western Union, Money Gram or other wire services, bank transfers, credit cards, PayPal and e-gold. With two cards from the same bank you can even do card to card transfers which further hide the movement of funds. With the addition of direct deposit or bill pay features, these cards typically have bank routing numbers and account numbers on them, so they appear to be legitimate bank accounts. Unlike bank accounts, however, they are easily acquired, and when used by a skilled cyber criminal, untraceable. Typically these cards require no identification, and there is no verification of any information provided. Additionally, these cards allow for transfers, known as loads, of up to $15,000 per day. Many also allow unlimited withdrawals. These cards are in such demand that they are often resold through eBay and other online services. Preloaded credit/debit cards have instilled such a level of safety, that some card holders will accept e-gold or other transaction onto their card and then deliver the money to its destination for a fee.

Later on in the book we will examine other interesting and creative ways to move money into and out of financial institutions, including via online games.

E-gold Primer

To understand account funding and money laundering, you must first fully understand how the virtual e-currency markets work. E-gold was the first digital currency provider, going online in 1996. The Gold & Silver Reserve, a private United States company, is the operator of the e-gold currency. The actual reserves are held by a trust, e-gold Ltd., based in the Caribbean island of Nevis. As of this writing there are approximately 2.8 million funded accounts, moving approximately two million dollars a day.[39] What makes e-gold unique, is that it is 100% backed at all times by gold bullion. In other words, actual gold is stored in secure vaults located in Canada and Dubai, certified by the London Bullion Market Association (LBMA), and held in trust for you. E-gold also operates and issues other e-metals, including e-silver, e-platinum, and e-palladium, which are all 100% backed by their respective metals. However, the most popular metal, by an overwhelming margin, is still e-gold.

E-gold allows for the instant transfer of gold ownership between two users. E-gold does not sell gold; you must use an independent digital currency exchanger to convert your local currency back and forth to gold. You would typically transfer money to the independent digital currency

---

39. e-gold. "e-gold Statistics." e-gold.com. http://www.e-gold.com/stats.html.

exchanger. The independent digital currency exchanger then purchases gold for your account and deposits it into a vault for a small fee. You then spend your money using electronic gold just as you would any other form of currency. The real gold never actually moves, it simply changes ownership, moving from one e-gold account to another. OmniPay, owned by e-gold, is just one example of a large number independent digital currency exchangers.

In April 2007, a federal grand jury indicted e-gold Ltd. and its owners on charges of money laundering, conspiracy, and operating an unlicensed money transmitting business.[40] To avoid charges, e-gold will likely fully cooperate with law enforcement, and possibly turn over their account database and IP history. E-gold may not be as anonymous as it once was, but it continues to offer some level of anonymity. Cyber criminals would likely rotate their IP address through anonymous proxies, the TOR or HaxTOR network, or BOTs for additional protection making it difficult for law enforcement to unravel the web, even with E-gold's cooperation.

Tools & Tips: The easiest way to defeat funding with stolen money is to wait until funds have

---

40. Krebs, Brian. "U.S.: Online Payment Network Abetted Fraud, Child Pornography." Washington Post. http://www.washingtonpost.com/wp-dyn/content/article/2007/05/01/AR2007050101291.html (accessed Jun. 14, 2007).

---

cleared before allowing trading from the account. Usually it is a business decision as to whether your company wants to allow immediate access to funds. With that being said, you may not be able to wait until those funds clear, which can take 5 days or more. Your firm will need to weigh the risk of potential loss, say for accepting and allowing the trading of money from a counterfeit cashier's check, against the benefit of allowing access to legitimate funds quickly. As far as detecting pre-pay cards, there is no effective method to do so at this point in time.

Staging the Account

Staging the account is a relatively easy process; even the novice cyber criminal rarely makes a mistake here. To properly set the dump account up, the cyber criminal will likely test fund transfers back and forth to their first intermediary, typically the preloaded credit card. These tests will establish money movement in this account and help bypass fraud systems that rely on anomaly detection. If the cyber criminal consistently moves a large portion of his funds back and forth, he should not trip any of these systems when he executes the pump-and-dump and needs to move funds out. The dumper will often buy and sell securities during this staging to establish a level of normal activity for the account. As anomaly detection systems become more sophisticated, it's likely the dumper will buy and sell the target security in advance of the pump-and-dump to fool such systems.

In summary, the financial institution has very few chances to identify the dumpers' account. New accounts that don't match the information returned by credit checks should be carefully watched. In addition, fund movement and peculiar trading patterns should raise suspicions. For example trades that make no sense, such as buying a stock on one day and selling within a few days on no news raise red flags. If the cyber criminal makes it past your detection, the account will most likely remain under the radar until after a pump-and-dump has taken place.

Terms

ACH – Automated Clearing House. ACH is an electronic network used for financial transactions.

Anomaly Detection – A computer system capable of unsupervised data mining. The result is a model that can identify data sets that deviate from the norm.

CAPTCHA – Completely Automated Public Turing Test to tell Computers and Humans Apart. Invented by Luis von Ahn, CAPTCHA is a challenge-response test designed to be easy for humans to solve, but difficult or computationally intensive for a computer.[41]

Digital Gold – A form of electronic currency denominated in gold weight, and backed by gold through unallocated or allocated gold storage.

Drops - Individuals who convert virtual money obtained in cyber crime to real cash. Drops often represent safe addresses for goods purchased or safe bank accounts for stolen money to be transferred into.

---

41. Thompson, Clive, "For Certain Tasks, the Cortex Still Beats the CPU," Wired Magazine, iss. 15.07, June 2007. http://www.wired.com/tech-biz/it/magazine/
15-07/ff_humancomp.

Firewall – A piece of software that inspects network traffic and permits or denies that traffic based on a set of rules.

Geolocation - The mapping of a device connected to the Internet to a geographic location based on the IP address of the device. Due to the nature of the Internet, as the location becomes more specific the accuracy drops.

Geocoding – The process of assigning geographic coordinates to other data records.

MAC Address – Media Access Control address. A MAC address is a unique hardware address assigned to the physical network card. It is possible to change MAC addresses on most network cards today.

NAT – Network Address Translation. NAT is a technique of re-writing the source and destination IP address in order to enable multiple host computers on a private network access to the Internet using a single public IP address.

NSA – National Security Agency. The NSA is a US government agency responsible for cryptological intelligence.

PII – Personally Identifiable Information. PII is any piece of information, or combination of pieces of information, that can be used to uniquely identify or locate a single person.

Proxy - A computer system or software designed to service the requests of other computers by forwarding requests to their destination, and returning responses to the proper requestor.

VerID – A commercial product available from RSA that incorporates knowledge-based authentication to provide real-time authentication of a customer.

CHAPTER 6 Acquiring Access to Accounts

I don't believe in psychology. I believe in good moves.

- Bobby Fischer

You are fortunate that unlike the late Bobby Fischer, the cyber criminal looks for "good enough" attacks, rather than the best move at every stage of the game. What is interesting about the "good enough" approach is that it causes cyber criminals and financial firms to form a strange, symbiotic relationship. If cyber criminals took the time and built a top-notch attack, it would be unlikely that a financial firm would be able to combat it in any effective timeframe. As a result, the cyber criminals could damage a company to the point of bankruptcy due to losses, bad press, and client perceptions. Instead, the "just okay" attacks have created an arms race, with neither side able to declare victory, but both sides feeding each other.

The easiest, and sometimes hardest, part of the pump-and-dump scam requires that the cyber criminal acquire enough account credentials to move the market in a particular security. Over the years, there have been multiple approaches to solving this problem. We will attempt to work through a large number of them in this chapter. Often, criminals rotate through these techniques and it's not unusual to see reuse of older, even less effective, techniques. The amount of work a cyber criminal puts in here is often reflected in the number of accounts acquires. Most readers of this book may not fully grasp the number of credentials that are stolen every day; the author of this book has witnessed a small attack against a financial institution that compromised over 0.7% of the institution's client base within one week. While that number seems small, it works out to 700 compromised accounts per 100,000 clients. That was just one attack utilizing a trojan and one back end server. At any given point in time there are tens of thousands of credential-stealing trojans in the wild. These trojans are stealing not only credentials to your site, but the credentials to every site your client interfaces with. Based on this one case, you shouldn't be surprised if 4% or more of your clients may have lost their credentials. Simply changing their passwords will result in the immediate loss of that new password. A professional cleanup is necessary to restore security on the user's computer.

Once a cyber criminal has successfully compromised a user's personal computer, he is provided with personal data such as account numbers, usernames, and passwords –any text a person might enter online. Using this information, cyber criminals can assume another's identity. Cyber criminals run up charges averaging $3,968 per victim in most industries, according to a Nationwide Mutual Insurance Co. survey.[42] However, when it comes to financial fraud against online brokers, the average attack is between $5,000 to $20,000 dollars. The ultimate damage though, is often much greater than the profit taken. Brokerage firms can end up holding millions of dollars of worthless

42. Brenner, Bill. "Hackers Installing Keyloggers at a Record Rate." Search Security.com. http://searchsecurity.techtarget.com/news/article/0,289142,sid14_gci1145229,00.html (accessed December 19, 2007).

securities. Once the pump-and-dump has started, legitimate day traders start to jump into the stock movement. After they realize that there is no news to justify the sudden gain in price and volume, a panic ensues, causing a stampede out of the position. This sudden sell-off causes more confusion and drives the stock price down even faster.

Understanding Credential Theft

To truly understand where the cyber criminals are lifting these credentials, we must explore the places where credential theft can occur in your system.

Due to modern malware utilizing multiple techniques it's often difficult to classify the malware or the attacks. For simplicity sake we put forth a simple classification scheme. It is as follows:

- Phishing/Vishing - any component with a primary attack vector between the user and the keyboard or dial-pad.

- Key logging - any component with a primary attack vector between the keyboard and the application, often a browser.

- Form grabbing - any component with a primary attack vector within or after the browser.

There are four major approaches to credential theft, listed in order of popularity.

The most popular method of credential theft involves a software attack. This attack may come in one of many forms: installation of a custom keyboard driver, the substitution of the filter driver in the keyboard stack, the interception of kernel functions through a variety of methods, the interception of certain DLL functions while in User Mode, or the requesting of information using undocumented APIs. Typically, the more complex the approach is, the less likely it is to be used in common trojan programs. Highly complex approaches generally appear in custom-designed trojan programs targeting financial data from a specific company. The bulk of all software attacks in the wild today involve keyloggers, and this book will focus on them. The basic concept behind a keylogger is to get between the user's fingertips and the submission of data to the web site in order to gain access to the user's credentials. Note that keylogging software and hardware are sold at many legitimate computer sites for policing children and spouses.

The second most popular method revolves around social engineering, requiring your customer to participate for the credential theft to occur. This method includes phishing and vishing attacks.

The third most popular method is an external attack. External attacks rely on additional factors such as hidden cameras and user observation, also known as shoulder surfing. While these techniques aren't frequently used, they still put in appearances, and you should pay attention to developments in this method.

Finally, the last method is a hardware attack. Hardware attacks involve adding a hardware device to the keyboard ports or the use of specially modified keyboards. Some hardware attacks even involve tapping the keyboard wiring or the computer system board. Hardware keyloggers are typically not used by cyber criminals due to the need to be physically present to install them.

Software Attacks

In this section we are going to explore various software attacks. The diagram below (Figure 6-1) shows places where a savvy cyber criminal can use malicious software to compromise user credentials.

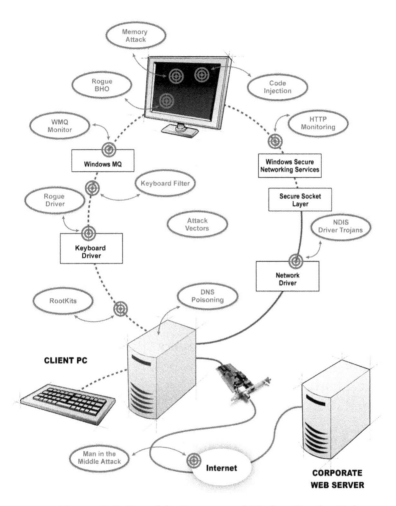

Figure 6-1 Possible Sources of Stolen Credentials

According to iDefense, cyber criminals are moving to keyloggers at an exponential rate; in the year 2000, criminals had launched just 300 unique keyloggers. By 2004, the number had increased to 3753 unique loggers. As of 2005, the figure had increased by 65 percent to 6191 unique loggers[43] (Figure 6-2).

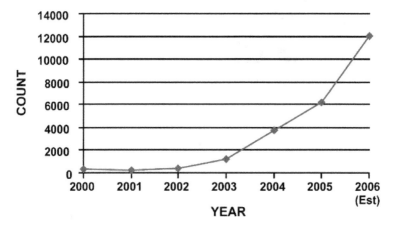

Figure 6-2 Pieces of Malware in the Wild Utilizing Key Logging Capabilities

Symantec recently issued a report that claims that almost 50% of the malicious programs detected during the past year are specifically intended to harvest personal user data.

SANS Institute released a report, conducted by John Bambenek, that claimed that approximately 10 million computers in the United States alone are currently infected with some form of malicious software with keystroke logging capability.

---

43. VeriSign, "iDefense Tracks Dramatic Growth in Password-Stealing Keyloggers," news release, November 15, 2005.

There are three main implementation methods used to build software keyloggers: a polling method, a system hook, and a filter driver. Most cyber criminals will attempt to maximize the amount of data captured by including multiple methods in a single piece of malware. The chart below shows the breakdown of the methods various keyloggers are using (Figure 6-3).

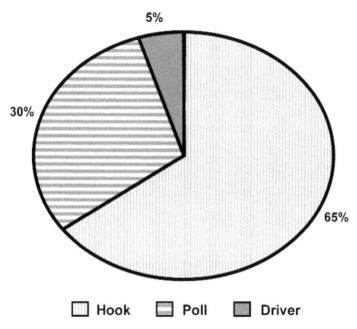

Figure 6-3 Methods Used in Software Key Loggers

Some of the more prevalent pieces of malware with key logging capability include Haxdoor, A311 Death, and Backdoor-BAC. Configuration tool kits are now available. Malware itself continues to grow in sophistication with the addition of rootkit capabilities. Creation toolkits are sold online for a mere $200 to $500, depending on specifications. These tool kits allow even an amateur script kiddie to craft a very dangerous piece of malware. Below is a screen shot of a typical keylogger's configuration screen (Figure 6-4).

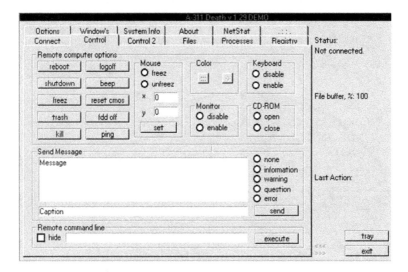

Figure 6-4 Control Screen of a Trojan

The toolkit above includes the ability to disable firewalls, target specific sites, and inject code into the victim's browser.

Often, malicious software is installed via the "drive-by" install. In this type of install the cyber criminal places the malicious code on a web site. When a user browses to the site, the malicious software uses a security flaw to install on the target machine. Some of the less popular methods for distribution include email, peer-to-peer, instant messaging, and compromised shareware and free-ware programs. Google recently surveyed 4.5 million web sites and found that 450,000 of those sites had malicious software waiting to perform a drive-by install. Another 700,000 sites were flagged as suspicious but with a slightly lower confidence.[44]

As recently as November of 2007, Google found its search engine seeded, known as SEO poisoning, with tens of thousands of pieces of malware. Users with vulnerable systems that visited these malicious web pages from Google could acquire a piece of malware known as Scam.Iwin. This malware was designed to use the victim's computer to defraud Google and its advertisers; however it would have been just as easy for the cyber criminals to install malware with a keylogger.[45]

Rootkits

In recent years there has been a large increase in rootkits, malicious software that protects itself using stealth techniques. Rootkits can often sneak under the radar of anti-virus software and evade detection for long periods of time. Many people

44. Provos, Niels, McNamee, Dean, Mavrommatis, Panayiotis, Wang, Ke, and Modadugu, Nagendra. "The Ghost In the Browser Analysis of Web Based Malware." Google, Inc. http://www.usenix.org/events/hotbots07/tech/full_papers/provos/provos.pdf (accessed Jan. 21, 2007).
45. Claburn, Thomas. "Google Purges Malware Sites Targeting Searchers." InformationWeek, November 27, 2007. http://www.informationweek.com/news/internet/showArticle.jhtml?articleID=204300556.

are confused by the term rootkit; a rootkit is not malware, it is simply a method used to hide malware. There are two techniques currently in use today, User Mode or Kernel Mode. In the countermeasures section of the book we will look at ways to detect these root kits or render them ineffective.

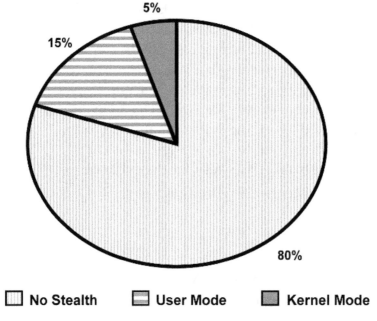

Figure 6-5 Types of Stealth Utilized by Malware

Most software utilizing stealth techniques utilizes User Mode, or a combination of Kernel Mode and User Mode. Kernel Mode stealth is almost always seen with some form of User Mode component (Figure 6-5). Choosing a stealth technique creates a dilemma for the cyber criminal. The abilities of the User Mode applications are limited by the security rights granted to the user. The User

Mode applications that are needed by the Kernel portion of the rootkit may not be present or accessible on the victim's system. In addition, hiding your root kit becomes a major issue since User Mode operations are far easier to detect than Kernel Mode operations. However all is not lost. Research is progressing rapidly and as early as 2006, a student produced an IRCBot that ran only in Kernel Mode. Further development will lead to complete Kernel Mode rootkits capable of logging keystrokes, bypassing system firewalls, and remaining completely undetectable.[46] Interestingly, a pure Kernel Mode rootkit would miss auto-complete passwords as this data is passed in the application layer.

Some of the most popular root kits, more proof of concept than anything else, include:

NTRootkit was released by Greg Hoglund in 1999. It was the first Windows rootkit. It can hide files and directories, registry keys, windows processes, and record keystrokes. It also had some capabilities to encrypt traffic and move data off the infected machine.

EeyeGootRoot was released by the Eeye team. It was the first BIOS NDIS rootkit, which meant it could theoretically load from any bootable device

46. Tibbar, Adventures of the White Rabbit. http://tibbar.blog.co.uk/2006/04/06/
kernel_mode_IRCbot~708256.

or media. It would then hook and patch OSLOADER during the boot, loading underneath the OS.

FU was released by James Butler, aka Fuzen. It is a very sophisticated rootkit which uses kernel data modification directly in memory (DKOM). While this rootkit is quite large, it could be modified for use in the wild. It can hide processes, elevate process privileges, and make forensics is impossible by interfering with the Windows Event Viewer. FU can even hide device drivers without any form of hooking.

Some popular rootkits that have been seen in the wild include:

ByShell, a Chinese rootkit released by Baiyuanfan. At the time, it implemented a brand new technique for hiding TCP connections by hooking asynchronous I/O calls.

He4Hook, a popular open source Russian rootkit based on hooking, it requires only minimal skill to use. It can hide processes and files.

Vanquish, based on a Romanian rootkit, Vanquish was released by Xshadow around 2003. It is based on DLL injection, making it is extremely small in size and ideal for malware. It can hide files, folders, and registry entries, and collect login information.

HackerDefender, also known as HxDef and coded by Holy Father, is well known in rootkit circles. It is relatively small in size, taking less than 1 second to install its driver and service. HackerDefender was viewed as such a large threat that it is included in Microsoft's top 21 threats list. It is probably the most popular rootkit in existence due to the following "features:" a backdoor in the code, a highly flexible configuration file, command line setup options, and, best of all, remote installation.

Rogue Driver

A rogue keyboard driver is a specialized keyboard driver that operates at the kernel level and receives data directly from the input device. In this attack, the malicious driver replaces a portion of the core software for interpreting keystrokes. Rogue drivers can remain nearly undetectable by taking advantage of the fact that they are executed on the boot of the operating system, before any user-level applications start. This method has not been witnessed in the wild yet due to the amount of knowledge needed to execute it successfully; in addition, keyboard drivers tend to be hardware specific. With the right skills, a cyber criminal may be able to create a generic driver by reverse engineering and modifying a commercial one, however testing becomes a major obstacle. As with the root kit, since the driver runs at the kernel level, it will fail to capture auto-complete passwords. There may be growth in the use of rogue drivers as other avenues are closed to cyber criminals over the next few years.

Keyboard Filter

A keyboard filter is a piece of code that sits above the keyboard driver and adds some additional functionality to the device without altering the original driver. Most users are not aware that they legitimately use keyboard filters on a daily basis. Originally, keyboard filters were used to extend the functionality of the PC through the use of hotkeys; other keyboard filters were designed to toggle between keyboard layouts, such as the popular program Keyboard Ninja. Still other valid keyboard filters allow companies to track employee activity throughout the workday, or allow users to track the activity of a third party while using their computer. Often, legitimate software and techniques are used by cyber criminals to deliberately steal a users' confidential information. While keyboard filters have been around for quite a while, the growth of their use for nefarious purposes has kept pace with the rapid increases in spam and spyware. The numbers vary greatly depending on which study you believe, but no matter which study you follow, the message is clear, keylogger use by cyber criminals is on the rise.

Windows API

System hooks, known as hooking, require more skill as a programmer and involve using the Microsoft Windows API. Hooking is a technique for gaining control over a particular piece of code execution. Microsoft actively uses hooking techniques in their debugging and tracing tools. Hooking provides a mechanism that can easily alter the behavior of the operating system and 3rd party applications, without access to the source code. Hooking has so many legitimate, if poorly thought out uses, that it is not going away. It was designed to not only contribute to advanced functionalities, but also to inject user-supplied code for debugging purposes. Unfortunately, hooking is now utilized by the majority of cyber criminals today. Malicious code typically uses the Windows API known as SetWindowsHookEx(), in conjunction with additional parameters, to create hooks that can monitor all keystrokes. A keylogger that creates a hook using this Windows function is also capable of capturing auto-complete passwords. This method is often popular in commercial software keyloggers such as Blazing Tools Perfect Keylogger, Spector, Invisible Keylogger Stealth, and Keysnatch. Hook-based keyloggers can be defeated with anti-keylogging software that blocks the passing of control from one hooked procedure to another. Some of the other popular APIs to hook include send, connect, CryptDeriveKey, CyptImportKey, CryptGenKey, HttpOpenRequestW, InternetReadFileExA, InternetReadFileExW, CommitUrlCacheEntryA,

InternetReadFile, InternetQueryDataAvailablility, HttpOpenRequestA, HttpSendRequestA, HttpSendRequestW, GetClipboardData, DispatchMessageA, DispatchMessageW, ExitProcess. For more specific information about these APIs please reference the Microsoft web site.

A second method of key logging uses polling, and is perhaps the easiest to code. Commonly, this method is used by low level cyber criminals with very little coding experience. The malicious code is commonly written in Visual Basic or Borland Delphi. This method involves writing a small piece of code that simply checks the current state of the keyboard, utilizing either GetAsyncKeyState or the GetKeyboardState. It continuously loops checking for key presses. The disadvantage to this method is that since it polls, it may miss characters. To get all the characters, the polling must occur at high speed, taxing the CPU and raising the likelihood of detection. Cyber criminals using these techniques typically do not have the skill set required to hide the running polling processes, making long term detection a near certainty.

Below are just some of the more common APIs that cyber criminals are using today in malware. For additional information, reference Microsoft's developer documentation.

Polling Methods

GetKeyState returns the current state for a given key on the keyboard. You pass the function the key you are interested in and it returns a value letting you know if the key is being pressed or not. It does not require administrator privileges. Although stealthier than a global hook, it is less reliable.

GetAsyncKeyState is similar to GetKeyState, except it returns not only the current state of the given key; it also returns the state of the key since the prior call. This polling method is more reliable than GetKeyState, since any key missed could be caught by this API. It's also possible that multiple keys may have been pressed, and the recorded order could be incorrect. Like the prior method, this method does not require administrator privileges.

GetKeyboardState returns the current state of all keys on the keyboard in one call. This polling method returns information on which keys are being pushed at the instant of the call. Like the methods above, GetKeyboardState does not require administrator privileges.

Hooks

SetWindowsHookEx is a low level keyboard hook usually used with the WH_KEYBOARD_LL parameter. This hook monitors low level keyboard input. The hook doesn't require a DLL, so nothing needs to be injected into another process. Administrative privileges are not required.

The SetWindowsHookEx can also be used with the WH_JOURNALRECORD parameter to create a journal record hook. As with the above hook, no DLL is required and no administrative privileges are needed.

Other Methods

GetRawInputData is similar to a hook, since it works without the need to poll. As the name implies, this API reads the raw keyboard data from the device.

DirectInput is a function contained within the DirectX suite. DirectInput is typically used by video games to monitor your keyboard. Currently there is no malicious software utilizing this method however it's just a matter of time. This API doesn't require administrator privileges.

WMQ Monitoring

Windows interacts with other components through the use of Windows messages and Windows message queues. A skilled cyber criminal can listen to the various message queues and intercept keyboard data as it is passed around between these components.

Rogue BHO

The rogue BHO, one of the more popular methods of keystroke logging, involves grabbing form data with a browser helper object (BHO) in Internet Explorer or Cross Platform Component Object Models (XPCOM) in Firefox. A BHO or XPCOM is essentially a form of code injection. The BHO or XPCOM were originally designed to extend browser functionality and allow seamless integration with the underlying browser engine. Unfortunately, in this configuration the BHOs and XPCOMs can circumvent any SSL encryption on a website, and can read user ids, passwords, or any other web form information.

Most people have heard of exploits utilizing BHOs. Most users think they are safe from these exploits by using Mozilla Firefox. Unfortunately, they have a false sense of security. Almost any malicious extension that can be written as a BHO extension can also be written as an XPCOM extension. In March of 2006, an XPCOM extension known as JS.Ffsniff, a piece of JavaScript that uses XPConnect, was discovered in the wild. XPConnect, is a JavaScript interface that allows access to XPCOM objects. JS.Ffsniff would capture user credentials and mail them to a specific email address. More recently, an XPCOM extension called Infostealer.Snifula used an almost identical approach. Infostealer.Snifula took the attack a step forward by listening to not only form submit events but also form click events. It would then collect all form fields, forward them to the main process and send the information back to the attacker.

To see what a BHO or an XPCOM object-based attack can extract from a form, download one of several legitimate products that display exactly what is contained in a form. Some of the more popular extensions are IE DOM Inspector for Internet Explorer, Web Developer Toolbar for Firefox and DOMSpy for either.

Memory Attack

Direct memory attacks are very rare, and as such are more theoretical. The inability to guarantee that a process will allocate the same memory space to keystroke or form data each time it launches renders these attacks difficult to implement. This attack requires that you locate keystroke or form data, while it is in memory, before it is sent to the web server. Once located, you can directly access the underlying memory assuming that you can bypass any memory protection. While difficult, this attack may become more prevalent in the future. There are already several examples in the wild of hooking the memory manager.

Code Injection

The most complex and stealthiest trick in the cyber criminal's arsenal involves code injecting key processes or dynamic link libraries (DLL) in the browser. Code injection is quite complex, and the technical details are out of scope for this book. We will very briefly touch on the techniques that can be used to inject your code into the browser.

The first technique involves placing code into a DLL and then mapping the remote process via window hooks. Typically, the malicious code would consist of a hooking engine; the hooking engine is responsible for performing the injection into the desired process and receiving status information from the DLL component. The second piece would be the driver module, which is responsible for performing the credential interception.

The second technique is to place code into a DLL and to map the DLL into the process using LoadLibrary and CreateRemoteThread. Again, this method would likely have a similar hooking engine and driver module component.

The third technique is to copy code into the process directly using WriteProcessMemory and to start the execution with CreateRemoteThread.

The advantage of code injection is that once injected, anything the malicious code does appears to be coming from the injected process. In other words, if Internet Explorer is successfully injected, the malicious code can send data out port 80 under the auspices of the Internet Explorer process. Since most users browse the Internet, the malware author could remain hidden from most firewalls but still send out data. As Software as a Service (Saas) takes over, the threat grows.

HTTP Monitoring

HTTP monitoring is similar to BHOs in the sense that you can grab anything on a form before SSL encryption takes effect; HTTP monitoring is currently a very popular form of attack. Often, monitoring programs are marketed as form grabbers. Form grabbers are often confused with keyloggers. Although both wind up with users credentials, form grabbers tend to be more resource efficient than keylogger technology. The ability to grab only targeted information, instead of every keystroke typed, allows monitors to scale better in larger implementations. Often, form grabber trojans are packaged with keystroke logging technology as a backup. A quick search on the Internet will lead you to many form grabbing programs, available for purchase that can easily create malicious trojans capable of bypassing SSL security and stealing user ids and passwords. One example is Rat Systems (www.ratsystems.org). Please note that this site is not trustworthy, and you probably don't want to visit it. Below is a description of some of the technology available at the site (Figure 6-6).

IE Form Grabber

This technology allow to collect web data form. This technology allows you to collect forms with authorization based on magicword [sic] used in United kingdom and other EU countries. Module can collect data from browser even if connection is secured and data transmitted thru HTTPS protocol. This technology used in UK Banks authorization leak test.

Saved Passwords Grabber: Protected Storage, Outlook, Far FTP, TotalCommander FTP, The Bat!

This is a module for retrieving passwords from system. Almost all passwords, stored in system (cashed [sic] passwords, autocomplete forms, outlook, The Bat! And others) can be founded [sic]

E-Gold Grabber

Old technology which is now in review and rewriting stage. It shows how it's easy to grabb [sic] passwords typed even with SRK (Secure randomized keyboard).

Figure 6-6 Technology Available for Purchase at RatSystems.com

As you can see, these applications are available; they have been for years, and on a number of sites.

Carder forums have plenty of links for every level of experience. Forums present tutorials on form grabbers, guides to writing them, and copies of form grabber source code. Forums even provide complete tool kits. The important question has gone from "Do you have the skills?" to "How much are you willing to pay?"

Some popular form grabbing trojans are Apophis, HaXdoor, Nuclear Grabber, PRG, and Qbot. In a later chapter we will examine PRG/NTOS in detail. This particular trojan is notable for its ability to evade most anti-virus vendors.

Tools & Tips: In theory, form grabbers are easy to defeat. Prior to posting form data, encrypt the form data using both a rotating encryption key and algorithm. Then have a backend server piece that can specify the encryption key and algorithm, and decrypt the data. In this scenario, the form grabber would only be able to grab encrypted fields. This change would force attackers to either build specific malware for your domain or to move to other attack methods. This method would also have the added benefit of defeating any man-in-the-middle type attacks like those executed against CitiBank's 2-factor system, since the credentials passed to the new site would not be properly encrypted, adding more problems for the cyber criminal to overcome.[47]

---

47. Krebs, Brian. "Citibank Phish Spoofs 2-Factor Identification" Washington Post. http://blog.washingtonpost.com/securityfix/2006/07/citibank_phish_spoofs_2factor_1.html (accessed January 30, 2009).

NDIS Driver

The Network Driver Interface Specification (NDIS) has two basic functions. First, it manages a network adapter, sending and receiving data. Second, it interfaces with higher-level drivers, such as intermediate drivers and transport protocol drivers. While this driver could not steal encrypted data, it would have access to any unencrypted data.

All of these software techniques would likely encrypt stolen data at the lowest possible level and then attempt to move it via various techniques. One of the best ways to move the data is to post the encrypted data in the URL using the GET method. For example, instead of using a POST command to post EncryptedUserA, EncryptedPasswordB to malicious-site.com, the cyber criminal could move the data with the GET method. The cyber criminal could execute a GET method to MaliciousSite.com/app?EncryptedUserA&EncryptedPasswordB with the same end result. Ideally the encrypted userid and password would be concatenated to look less suspicious. Currently the weakness the cyber criminals have is that they have been encrypting stolen data using a simple substitution cipher such as ROT 13 or obfuscation via bitwise XOR. It's likely that they will recognize this weakness and move to more secure algorithms such as 3DES and AES.

This technique could be extended further by creating what appeared to be let's say a legitimate photo sharing site. The attacker could request a specific picture with the encoded user id and password. If someone later attempted to investigate the GET statement, the malicious site could return an actual picture, leading investigators to believe the site and GET was legitimate.

Most web traffic is composed of GET methods rather than POST methods. In some situations, companies restrict the POST method. Using GET conceals credential theft in a sea of activity. This camouflage is critical, as the longer a cyber criminal can conceal his presence, the more victims he can compromise. Another creative way to move data would be to use name service queries, though large numbers of them may cause suspicion.

Social Engineering Attacks

Social engineering involves manipulating a user into giving up his personal information. We will touch on the wide variety of social engineering techniques beginning to appear in the wild. Due to its prevalence, however, we will focus most of our attention, on phishing.

Phishing

Phishing is such a huge topic that it has a chapter dedicated to it later in the book. Basically, phishing is an attempt to steal a person's credentials by impersonating a legitimate site or email address. Phishing usually starts with an email that contains links, and those links connect to a replica of a trusted web site.

IVR/Vishing

Interactive Voice Response (IVR) attacks are relatively new, but are growing in popularity. The cyber criminal replicates the IVR system of the target company and sets up a toll free number for it. The criminal then send out emails to clients asking the user needs to call in. At some point during the call, the user is asked to enter account number and pin information.

Trojan Horse

A trojan horse, as explained earlier in this book, is a malicious application disguised as something desirable, such as the latest game, or a hacked copy of an office application. Once opened by the user, the malware is installed on the user's computer.

Road Apple

A road apple is a variation of the trojan horse attack. The cyber criminal leaves tempting physical media around, hoping a curious user will insert into his or her personal computer. The media may be in the form of CD-ROMs, floppy disks, or USB flash drives. The criminal relies on the auto-run feature of Windows to automatically install his malware onto the victim's computer.

External Attacks

External attacks are rare, as they typically require either physical proximity or elaborate setup on the part of the cyber criminal. Out of all external attacks, shoulder surfing is the most common one that you will see.

Audio Recording

This attack is more theoretical than practical. Audio recording attacks are best suited for Internet cafes, libraries, or other kiosk locations. The steals credentials simply by listening to a user type on a keyboard. Li Zhuang, Feng Zhou, and Doug Tygar have published a paper showing that if you have an audio recording of a user typing on a keyboard for a minimum of ten minutes, you can derive the typed content with a very high accuracy.[48] Different keys tend to make slightly different sounds. Although you don't know in advance which keys make which sounds, you can use machine learning to map keys based on language letter frequencies. While you may think that a large number of key-

---

48. Zhuang, Li, Zhou, Feng, and Tygar, Doug, "Keyboard Acoustic Emi-nations Revisited," 12th ACM Conference on Computer and Commu-nications Security, University of California at Berkley, pp. 373-382, Nov. 2005.

strokes would be required to derive the letters, it turns out it's far fewer than you might think.

Hidden Cameras

Hidden cameras are another avenue for attack in public places. Simply hiding a camera above a keyboard allows an attacker to collect all the information he needs. The effort required to translate a video feed to text does take some work, however. Once a camera is set up, it could transmit across the Internet, allowing the cyber criminal an added measure of safety. Some libraries use cameras to deter porn surfing, if these cameras happen to be Internet enabled it's possible a cyber criminal is already eavesdropping on the feed.

Shoulder Surfing

Shoulder surfing is an attack method that derives keystrokes from direct observation, usually by looking over the victim's shoulder. It can be accomplished from a distance using binoculars or other vision enhancing tools. Shoulder surfing is particularly easy in crowded places, as the cyber criminal is unlikely to be noticed. Shoulder surfing from a distance, while more difficult, is even harder to detect. After all, you are unlikely to think someone is stealing your credentials when you are sitting on the 5th floor of a hotel room. Simply cupping your hands over your keyboard, or using a piece of paper to obscure the entry of your credentials, is enough to defeat this low-tech attack.

Hardware Attacks

Keyloggers that fall under the hardware category are usually very small devices placed between the keyboard and the computer. In some instances, these devices can be placed within a cable or the computer itself. Of course, this type of device could also appear as a custom keyboard with a keylogger installed, such as those available from KeyGhost. With the continued advancement of miniaturization, hardware key loggerscan go undetected for long periods of time. These devices can capture thousands of keystrokes over time, including usernames, passwords, and email addresses. Unfortunately for the cyber criminal, these devices require physical access to install and retrieve. However, the latest generation of hardware keyloggers has the capability to interface with software on the PC and send the results out over networks. Of course, this increased convenience could lead to detection. There are no methods to detect these devices other than physical inspection, but there is some theoretical work being done to detect hardware keyloggers by measuring voltage drain on the keyboard connection.

Tools & Tips: The easiest way to defeat hardware keyboard loggers is to switch to an encrypting wireless keyboard. Today, only Bluetooth offers de facto encryption in this technology; check all other wireless systems for proper encryption before using them, as many keyboards have been cracked.[49] Even Bluetooth has known weaknesses, so be sure your firmware is up to date.[50] Of course all of this assumes that the manufacturer of one of these devices has not been compromised.

---

49. Moser, Max, and Schrodel, Philipp, "27Mhz Wireless Keyboard Analysis Report aka 'We know what you typed last summer'." Dreamlab Technologies, 2007.

50. McCormick, John. "Encryption takes a hit as new flaws surface in Bluetooth and AES." TechRepublic Website. http://articles.techrepublic.com/5100?1009_11?5737759.htm. (accessed July 29, 2007).

Terms

API – Application Program Interface. An API is an interface that allows one program to communicate with another program.

Bluetooth – It is a specification for wireless personal area networks. Bluetooth provides a way for portable devices to communicate securely at ranges up to 100 meters.

BHO – Browser Helper Object. A BHO is a plug-in in the form of a DLL module for Microsoft Internet Explorer designed to provide additional functionality to the browser. A BHO allows access to the Document Object Model (DOM) of the current web page and allows for control of navigation.

BIOS – Basic Input/Output System. The BIOS is the firmware code that runs when your PC is first turned on. Its purpose is to identify hardware and launch a more robust operating system.

Bitwise XOR – It is a simple symmetric cipher. The XOR or exclusive OR is a logical operation that results in a value of true if only one of the operands has a value of true.

Code Injection – The introduction, or injection, of computer code into another computer program which alters its execution.

DLL – Dynamic-link Library. A DLL is a library of functions that can be loaded and executed by other programs dynamically at run time.

Drive By Install – Also known as a drive by download, a drive by install is any download that occurs without the user's knowledge. This install may occur when the user visits a website or views an e-mail. Typically the install occurs through the exploitation of a bug in the browser, e-mail client or the operating system itself.

Filter Driver – A driver that adds additional functionality to a device, a filter driver may sit above or below the primary device driver.

Kernel Mode – A privileged mode, also referred to as system mode. Kernel Mode is one of two possible and distinct modes of operation of a CPU. Software operating in Kernel Mode is trusted and allowed to execute any instruction and reference any memory location. In this mode the executing software has complete control over all aspects of the computer.

Keyboard Driver – A computer program that interacts directly with the keyboard hardware and hides the complexity of the keyboard by exposing a simplified programming interface to other programs.

NDIS – Network Driver Interface Specification. NDIS is a programming interface for network cards developed jointly by 3Com Corporation and Microsoft.

Phisher – A person that engages in phishing by masquerading as a trusted entity in an attempt to fraudulently acquire sensitive information, such as usernames, passwords and credit card details.

Phishing - The impersonation of a trusted entity in order to acquire sensitive information from an end user.

Rootkit – A software package designed to seize unrestricted control of a computer operating system without authorization. Rootkits attempt to hide their presence on the system through the use of various methods. The term comes from the Unix world, where root is the unrestricted user.

ROT13 – A form of encryption known as a Caesar cipher, named after Julius Caesar, who used this simple encryption technique to communicate with his generals. ROT13 is a substitution cipher in which each letter is replaced by a letter located thirteen positions down the alphabet. For example, A is replaced with N. ROT13 is commonly chosen since performing ROT13 on the encrypted text gets you back to the original unencrypted text. ROT13 is considered weak because it succumbs to brute force and to frequency analysis of the letters.

SEO Poisoning – Search Engine Optimization Poisoning. SEO Poisoning is the process of improving one's search engine ranking though flaws in the search engine algorithms.

Spear Phishing – A phishing attack that specifically targets one organization or group.

TCP – Transmission Control Protocol. TCP provides guaranteed, in order delivery, of packets of data. It is responsible for segmenting data to fit into packets, and for controlling the rate at which the messages are sent.

User Mode – A non-privileged mode in which most programs run. In this mode, programs cannot access portions of memory that have been allocated to other programs. When a program is operating in User Mode, it is not trusted and is limited to a set of interfaces. User Mode programs have access to only portions of memory.

Vishing - The impersonation of a trusted entity utilizing VoIP technology in order to acquire sensitive information from an end user. Typically the attacker creates a replica of the target's voice prompt system and convinces unsuspecting users to input account numbers and pins.

CHAPTER 7 Executing the Dump

The quickest way of ending a war is to lose it.

- George Orwell

Assuming the prior steps outlined in this book have occurred successfully, and the cyber criminal remains undetected, he is now ready for the money-making part of his scam. At this point, the dumper's account has been properly vetted and is ready to go. The dumper now needs to select a security and start acquiring a position in it. The dumper's target security choice depends on the specifics of the attack and how much equity he controls in the pump accounts. The dumper always buys the target security in advance, and may or may not place limit orders in advance of the pump. Placing limit orders is a potential risk. They reduce the number of steps the dumper needs to take to profit, but they can also be a dead giveaway that his account is a dump account.

Tools & Tips: It may be possible to detect a dumper account by flagging any account that sets up multiple limit orders in a low volume security that are sufficiently away from the current asking price. While the false positive rate may vary significantly from institution to institution, it's worth investigating.

To be successful, the dumper needs to control more buying power than there is liquidity on the market for the selected security. For example, if stock symbol XYZ typically has orders open for 2000 shares at $1 at the time of day the dumper will strike, then the attacker needs a minimum of $2000 of buying power in the pump accounts to sweep the orders off the market and control the price.

Once the existing orders have been met, the dumper controls the price and can now place orders at whatever price he wants. At this point, the dumper controls significantly more buying power as investors will be buying and selling into the price move. This phase is a risky one, as the participation of other investors could cost the dumper control of the direction of the price movement. If the dumper is willing to take a risk in the loss of control, he can provide interest in the stock by performing wash trades. A wash trade is a trade where the cyber criminal sells the security he is pumping and then repurchases it back in the same account or a different account. While this trade doesn't move the price, it does artificially elevate the volume and creates the appearance of interest in the security. This sudden change will typically catch the attention of day traders. Once enough interest exists, the cyber criminal could start to pump up the stock and may not need to clear the order book as long as other day traders jump on the bandwagon. The end result would be a lower profit for the cyber criminal, but a profit nonetheless. There are a handful of attack types, and different amounts of buying power are needed for each.

The Pink Sheet and Bulletin Board Attack

The Pink Sheet and Bulletin Board attack is the most prevalent attack today, since it requires only a basic understanding of the market, and a minimal amount of buying power in the pump accounts. In this scenario, the dumper looks for Bulletin Board or Pink Sheet securities that trade low daily average volumes. The lower the volume and price of the security, however, the more likely the dumper is to be detected and shut down. The target won't necessarily be a rock bottom volume security, nor will it be at a rock bottom price.

Once the dumper has chosen and purchased the target security, he now sweeps all open orders off the order book by placing multiple buy orders in pump accounts. Once the order book is cleared, the dumper will use his pump accounts to put in buys at inflated prices. Since the book is cleared, the dumper can essentially set the price of the stock and its future short-term direction. Eventually the security's prices will cross the limit orders that have been placed in the dumper's account, allowing the dumper to profit.

Tools & Tips: Using a review and release mechanism, carefully inspect large market orders in low volume securities. The dumper, in his rush to clear the order book, will use market orders or limit orders that are far from the asking price for the security. It should be relatively straightforward to build an alert system to look for these anomalies.

There are some additional timing attacks that potentially make Pink Sheet/Bulletin Board attacks more devastating. A dumper could time his attacks to coincide with popular vacation weeks when financial services' fraud groups may be thinly staffed, such as the day after Thanksgiving, the week between Christmas and New Years day, etc. These could be challenging times for any firm, and present considerable opportunities for the cyber criminal.

The chief benefit of this attack is that it requires a relatively small investment in the dumper's account, and it requires only a small amount of equity in the pump accounts to move the price significantly.

The Option Attack

The Option Attack is almost identical to the Pink Sheet and Bulletin Board attack, however it deals specifically with options. The use of options has added advantages and disadvantages for both the dumper and the financial institutions on the pump side of the transaction.

As with the Pink Sheet and Bulletin Board attack, the attacker will look for options that are relatively cheap. The attacker then purchases puts or calls and attempts to manipulate the market to his advantage. The upside for the cyber criminal is that he can pick an option significantly out of the money, with no open interest. The lack of interest allows the dumper to set the price without having to clear an order book. This attack takes very little equity on the pump side to pull off, often less than an attack on Pinks Sheets or Bulletin Board stocks.

The downside in this attack for the financial institution is three-fold. First, when an option collapses there is often little if any residual value to the option, making the loss to the financial institution greater than with a stock. Second, it's difficult to break these trades due to the way the option market works. Third, it is possible to manipulate any company's options, regardless of size, by selecting options that are extremely out of the money. The shorter the time to the option's expiration, the more money the firms holding the pump side accounts will likely loose.

Fortunately, there is some upside for the financial institutions. First, it should be easy for a firm to build an alert system based on time to expiration and the volatility of the underlying security versus how far out of the money the option is. Second, options typically aren't automatically enabled in an account, making it more difficult for the dumper to locate suitable pump accounts.

The Pre/Post Market Attack

Pre/Post Market Attacks are really just Pink Sheet and Bulletin Board attacks with additional market timing built in. They get a separate category because there are some additional benefits and disadvantages for both parties involved.

For the dumper, the pre and post market session allows for a broader range of securities. Volume at this time of day is thin with most securities. Research has shown that very large companies are getting manipulated at these times of day. In addition to the low volume, most financial service firms do not maintain a twenty four by seven fraud group to monitor trades during these hours. The main downside to the dumper is that the low trade volumes quickly indicate where the dump side is, and who is on the other end of it.

For the financial firms, due to the low volume of trading in pre and post market hours, there are more automated tools at the typical firms' disposal. Firms can review a larger percentage of orders prior to hitting the market. Most financial firms simply tighten their trading rules as to what goes into review release. Although these rules are easily probed for thresholds, they can still reduce losses. Most pre and post market rules revolve around number of shares that one buyer can purchase in one trade, or they place a dollar cap on the total value of a trade. Usually, firms do not allow market orders during this time. The sudden arrival of a large number of market orders is a dead giveaway that something isn't correct. Be aware, though, that these types of systems can be an avenue for a denial of service attack, which may allow orders through.

The erroneous trade rule makes it easier for larger financial firms to break trades during the pre and post market sessions. During market hours, such trades are much harder to break. The erroneous trade rule was never intended to serve as a defense against lawbreakers. Instead, it was intended to catch trades that were clearly made in error. Still, the trading floors are more likely to allow you to use it during pre/post market sessions to break fraudulent trades

Listed Attacks

One type of attack quickly gaining ground is a variant of the Pink Sheet/Bulletin Board Attack. The Listed Attack is identical to the Pink Sheet/Bulletin Board Attack, however it involves low volume listed securities. Financial institutions should be aware of the Listed Attack, if they aren't already. Any security with a volume of less than one million shares a day or a price below $10 is at great risk for this type of attack. Additionally, any security that experiences predictable periods where its order book is small enough to be swept is also at risk for manipulation. With enough accounts and equity, a properly planned attack could manipulate companies that have even higher daily trade volumes and share prices.

Shorting Attacks

Additionally, listed stocks allow the attacker another interesting variation called the Shorting Attack. In this scenario, the attacker would short sell a given security in the compromised accounts, pushing the price of the security lower. The attacker could then purchase it in his own account at a discount. With no bad news on a quality listed stock it should quickly return to the pre-attack price and the attacker makes money. The benefit of this attack type is that the attacker could leave his money in his broker longer, further hiding his tracks. With a traditional pump-and-dump it's a matter of the SEC or FINRA blue sheeting a security. A blue sheet is a request to brokers for all accounts that transacted a given security. From this list, the authorities attempt to figure out who made what. Once they know who profited, they will start looking for accounts that turned around and cashed out quickly, a dead give away for the dumper. In the Shorting Attack, there is no rush for the attacker to move his money since the stock should naturally return to its normal daily trading range. This makes shorting attacks much tougher to track.

Timing Attack

The Timing Attack is another issue that may yet appear on the horizon. A timing attack would be a combination of any of the attacks above, combined with a slightly different technique. In order for the attacker to stay in the background, he would use a greater number of accounts. When launching his attack, he would place a single small order that falls below a broker's threshold for suspicion in each account. The orders would have the same impact on the security, however it would remain hidden until reported by the clients. This type of attack will likely appear before the end of 2008.

Initially it's likely the attacker would run serially through the pump accounts with a single trade to pump the stock. He would then repeat the process, continuing the sweep until all accounts were shut down. This approach allows the attacker to maximize his run up. Although the idea is simple, the actual attack requires precise timing, and requires full automation. One hurdle requires figuring out how many accounts are needed to pump a security by X%, though it's possible over time to get a near optimal solution through trial and error.

Destabilization Attack

An interesting theoretical attack would be the Destabilization Attack. The destabilization attack could ultimately be launched by protestors, activists or even terrorists. If a group was able to acquire a large number of accounts, they could target multiple securities and place small shorts in them. One account may place shorts in 10 different large companies for several thousand or tens of thousands of shares. While these trades wouldn't have an impact, imagine if thousands of accounts were compromised across brokerages, and all the trades were entered within minutes or seconds of each other. The result would be the possible destabilization of not only the companies under attack, but possibly even the destabilization of the markets. The attackers could cause further damage by using their compromised accounts to buy back the stock at a depressed value and then attempt to further short shares. Ultimately the broker would have to shut down any compromised user account. If the broker just shut down the affected symbols, the attackers could just launch another set of attacks later that day. Until the malware responsible was identified and a cleaning process developed, the owners of the compromised accounts would be required to enter orders via the phone with a broker. An attack like this may occur before the end of 2009. It's just a question of whether the attack will target an industry, like animal rights protestors targeting pharmaceutical companies, or target across industries, like terrorists attacking against multiple companies with the hope of destabilizing an entire market.

Terms

Blue Sheets – A request by the SEC for detailed information about trades performed by a firm and its clients. This information typically includes the security's name, date traded, price, transaction side and the parties involved. The term blue sheet comes from the fact that originally the requests were printed on blue paper. That system has been replaced by the electronic blue sheet system known as EBS.

Erroneous Trade Rule – Also known as NASD Rule 11890, it is a rule designed to allow for the breaking of trades that result from an obvious error. An example would be a broker placing a trade for 100,000 shares when he meant to enter 10,000. This rule is rarely allowed to be used to break fraudulent trades.

FINRA – Financial Industry Regulatory Authority. FINRA was formed by the consolidation of the enforcement arms of the NASD and the NYSE in 2007. FINRA provides regulatory oversight of all security firms that do business with the public.

Limit Orders – An order to buy a security at a specific price. A buy limit order will then execute at the specified price or lower, where a sell limit order will execute at the specified price or higher.

Listed Securities – Securities of companies that trade on an exchange, unlike unlisted securities, which trade in the over the counter markets.

Market Order – An order to buy or sell a given security at the current market price. During volatile times there is a greater chance of receiving a different price for parts of the order.

Option – A contractual agreement that allows the holder of the contract the option, but not the obligation, to buy or sell a security at an agreed upon price within a specified period of time.

Order book – An electronic "book" that contains a list of orders for a given security that have not been matched to a buyer or seller.

Out of the Money – In options trading, it is a call option whose strike price is higher than the current market price of the underlying security, or a put option whose strike price is lower than the current market price of the underlying security. These options are considered worthless.

Pre/Post Market Trading – Also known as extended hours, and after hours, the time when trading occurs outside the close of major U.S. exchanges. Currently, pre-market starts as early as 7:30am, and post-market goes as late as 8pm.

Shorting – The practice of selling securities that you do not own with the hope of repurchasing them at a later date and at a lower price. Shorting is a strategy that allows an investor to profit if a security goes down in price.

CHAPTER 8 Moving the Money Out

People who work sitting down get paid more than people who work standing up.

- Ogden Nash

In this chapter we will explore the numerous avenues the cyber criminals have to move their ill-gotten gains out of their dump account and into an account that they can convert into cash. Typically, cyber criminals will use one of two methods: method one is the money mule, usually an unsuspecting accomplice; method two is a direct transfer without a middle-man involved. Either way, the goal is to move the money as fast as possible, through as many systems as possible, to make the trail as tangled as possible, and perhaps not worth following.

Laundering Those Hard-Earned Dollars

Now that steps one through four are complete, the cyber criminal has just one last task left. Fortunately for him, customers are demanding greater access to their funds from their financial partners. To retain customers, and build larger feature sets than their competitors, financial institutions are more than happy to comply, benefiting the cyber criminal. Companies, such as Wells Fargo, Western Union, PayPal and e-gold, are in the business of helping customers move money from one location to another with just a few clicks of a mouse. Using rapid fund movement, cyber criminals can shorten the time a company has to identify and attempt to reverse a fund transfer. Some companies, like e-gold and others, do not even allow reversals.

The Mule

Cyber criminals recruit money mules, usually by convincing the mule that he is helping some overseas company expand their business into the United States by clearing funds quickly, or that the mule is performing a legitimate service. Typically the mule is lured in with a job scam; these jobs are pitched as "financial manager", "payment processor", "transaction specialist" or some other alluring title. Cyber criminals go to great lengths to recruit mules, since they are an important piece of the operation. Criminals do everything from creating legitimate looking web sites, conducting bogus interviews, etc. Mule recruiters have been seen recruiting in excess of 1300 mules per week. Recent research has revealed that cyber criminals have now been attempting to recruit mules via online dating sites. Cyber criminals even send the target flowers and notes to complete the illusion that the target is helping out a potential future mate.

Although there are many tactics for socially engineering the target into accepting the offer, the scam is always the same. The cyber criminal states that he will transfer a certain amount of money into the mule's bank account. The mule needs to forward a portion of the funds to an overseas location via Western Union, e-gold, PayPal or another cash delivery type method. Typically the ads state that the criminals will cover all transfer fees, and for their work the mule can keep a percentage of the funds. This payment to the mule is typically 3 to 10 percent of the total transfer amount. The services mentioned don't require detailed identification to pick up the funds, making them ideal candidates for "washing" the money. Below is an example of a typical recruitment email (Figure 8-1).

```
The young and perspective financial company
employs young experts. It is your unique
chance to start your career in the company
with a world name. We have some kinds of
vacancies. You can work freelance or work in
office. With us you can achieve new horizons
in your career. You can earn up to 3000-4000$
per month. The basic requirements to the can-
didates are: knowledge of PC and bases of
accounts department, honesty, clearness and
efficiency in work. If you are interested in
the given offer, please send your CV to
[removed]
```

Figure 8-1 Typical Mule Recruitment Email

Unfortunately, mule recruiters look for targets that are either not very sophisticated, desperate for work, or simply financially motivated. Victims typically work for minimum wage and are looking for ways to earn some spare cash. Once a mule has been brought into the fold, the recruiter will work closely with the mule via an instant messenger service. The recruiter will let the mule know when money will be arriving, and where it needs to go.

First money is transferred to a mule located in the same country as the financial institution. Typically, money is wired directly to the mule's bank account. Western Union is the preferred method for this first hop. The harder it is to pull back funds with a reversal, or get a trace; the more cyber criminal prefer that transfer method. The amount of the transfer to the bank account is based on the thresholds that the originating financial institution has in place. Most criminals attempt to send $5,000 or less to any one account. Once the cyber criminal has transferred the money, the clock starts ticking. The money must move as swiftly as possible. At this point, the recruiter will pressure the mule to get the money and wire it back out as quickly as possible; the recruiter will always place a sense of urgency on the transfer. The mule will now go to his bank and withdraw the cash. If the mule got this far, it is likely the cyber criminal will get his money as long as the mule acts quickly. The mule must keep the outgoing transaction amounts low in order to stay under the radar of the numerous systems that now come into play. These amounts range from a few hundred dollars up to $5,000. If more than $5,000 was taken from the financial institution, then the mule sends multiple wires, often to different accounts in different countries to increase the odds of success while at the same time increase the complexity of the investigation that is sure to follow. At this point, the mule is likely out of the money. He has wired off cash written against his account. Unfortunately for him, the inbound deposit may be reversed, leaving the mule poorer than when he started.

The next step involves yet another mule in yet another country. This next country is usually geographically close to the cyber criminal, though not always. Ideally, this mule lives in a country that doesn't cooperate quickly with the law enforcement in the originating country. This mule will then take the money he was wired from mule number one and turn it into virtual money (like e-gold). Once turned into virtual money, the trail is extremely difficult to follow. Many of these vendors require no proof of identity to set up an account. In addition, these transfers are typically one way so once here the money is effectively gone.

As you can see, the trail is getting very messy. The next step will send the virtual money to what is known as a "Wizard". The wizard is responsible for the final step - sending the money to an anonymous ATM account. The cyber criminal will get the anonymous ATM account in advance from someone he doesn't know. Alternatively the wizard creates the account using a fake address and name. The cyber criminal then removes his money using one or more ATM machines with no cameras. Sometimes mules are also used for this function, though the extra security is usually unnecessary. At this point the money has been successfully laundered, and there is no hope for the financial institution to retrieve it.

Liability to the Mule

Most mules are innocent victims that were duped into believing they were taking jobs with legitimate incomes from legitimate companies. Unfortunately for the mule, this belief does obviate the fact that he was part of an illegal money laundering operation. Law enforcement does not typically pursue criminal cases against mules, since they are usually unaware of the illegal nature of their work. Typically, the mule does not face charges as long as he cooperates with law enforcement and it can be shown that the mule was unaware of the scam.

Research has shown that not all mules are innocent; often the mule is willing to continue working an illegal job after negotiating a larger cut of the money.

Either way, it is possible for the financial institution to pursue a case against the mule, though winning such a case may not be straightforward. If a financial institution wants to pursue prosecution, the mule may be facing restitution, fines and/or jail time. In addition, most mules have low paying jobs; a successful judgment is unlikely to result in any additional fund recovery. Even worse, your company could increase damage to its brand by bringing cases like these before the public.

The Direct Move

Financial institutions that allow online bill payment need to pay special attention. While the traditional mule system requires multiple mules, an enterprising cyber criminal could take a more novel approach. The first step would be for the cyber criminal to open a pre-paid credit card. As discussed in an earlier chapter, pre-paid cards require no identity checks and offer bill paying and wire transfer capabilities. The second step would then involve moving money from the target financial institution to the card via bill pay, ACH, or wire transfer. This approach is very similar to how mules work. Once the funds have moved onto the pre-paid card, the criminal can then move them into an overseas account. A quick Google of "anonymous bank accounts" brings up a massive list of vendors. Most of these accounts are offshore in countries that have laws shielding the personal information of the holder of the account. From the anonymous account, the criminal can turn the funds into virtual money and head off to the wizard for final processing. The benefit of this method is that the money can move very quickly and potentially involve more hops, allowing even less time to freeze an account or stop payment.

Another variation involves wiring the money either to an offshore account or through a series of straw men and dummy corporations. This system doesn't look as suspicious, since money has been moving in and out of the account via the same account number as it has in the past. This method is a little more complex, and is often used by a cyber criminal who has partnered with traditional organized crime.

The Future of Laundering

As with everything, the fewer people involved the better. This aphorism also holds true for the cyber criminal. While mules are currently in use by multiple groups, they aren't necessary. Thousands of money laundering avenues are currently available for the creative cyber criminal. Any time there is a system on the Internet that allows for the low-cost movement of money, that system is subject to use by cyber criminals.

One interesting idea is to launder money through online games. There are now several games, including Entropia Universe and Second Life that allow in-game transfer from dollars to in-game currency and back again to dollars. Games, as a rule, are very low on law enforcement's radar. It would be easy to bill pay from the target's financial institution into one of these games, or perhaps wire to a pre-paid credit card and then move the currency into the virtual money of the game. Once in the game, there are numerous ways to launder the money. It can be moved around by virtual players, it can be traded for items that have worth in the game and can later be sold and converted back into cash. The most direct method would be to set up some sort of transaction with a group of players helping the cyber criminal. For instance, game players may create objects and sell them for what amounts to a few pennies in real money. The cyber criminal could purchase large quantities of these virtual objects, moving the money from one account to another without raising suspicion. Those players could then repeat the process, moving the money to an account held by the original cyber criminal. The cyber criminal then moves the money back to an anonymous ATM account and picks up his now laundered cash at a camera free ATM machine. Technically, this approach could occur in just about any game, including online poker sites. Any game can work, so long as the players aren't interested in winning or losing, but simply in washing the funds. As long as the attacker is literally everyone at the table, he can easily launder his money.

Terms

ACH – Automated Clearing House. ACH is
the name of an electronic network used
for financial transactions in the United
States. ACH processes large volumes of
batched transactions. Today, the total
value of ACH transfers amounts to tens
of trillions of dollars and billions of
transactions.

BillPay – A method that allows one to pay third
party bills electronically from his bank
account.

Mule – A person who transfers money or goods
to another country in return for a commission. Money mules serve as money
launderers and may or may not know
that they are supporting illegal operations.

PrePaid Credit Card – Also known as stored
value cards, these cards allow the card
holder spends money which has been
stored via prior deposits. Unlike a credit
card, prepaid cards are usually anonymous.

Wire – Wire Transfer, a method of transferring
money between two entities. Bank to
Bank wires are typically the safest, since
each account holder must have a proven

identity. Wires can be recalled for a short period of time. Wire transfers through cash offices are essentially anonymous. Once the money has been collected it cannot be recalled.

Wizard – A person that specializes in moving money to anonymous ATM accounts.

CHAPTER 9 Phishing

Feel the fear and do it anyway.

- Susan Jeffers

While the quote above may be out of context, it is the reason phishing works. Users want to believe that they know enough to spot a scam, or worse yet, they don't know anything and just click away. Phishing has been around for a long time. The first mention of phishing on the Internet goes back to January, 1996,[51] although the term itself first appeared in an earlier edition of the popular hacker magazine, 2600.[52] The article alluded to techniques to lure, or phish, for users' financial information and passwords. Phishing simply uses social engineering techniques to convince an end user to turn over his personal information, be that usernames, passwords, or credit card details.[53] Typically, a phisher gains access by masquerading as a source the user trusts. The phish usually starts with an email or an instant message to the user. The message directs the user to give details at a website, although phone numbers are now a growing trend. Even voice phishing, known as vishing, has started to appear.

One of the earliest known phishing attacks took place against America Online (AOL) during the

51. Oxford English Dictionary. "phish, v." OED Online. http://www.oed.com/.

52. Ollmann, Gunter. "The Phishing Guide: Understanding and Preventing Phishing Attacks." Whitepaper, NGSSoftware Insight Security Research, 2005. http://www.ngssoftware.com/papers/NISR-WP-Phishing.pdf.

53. Jakobsson, Markus, "The Human Factor of Phishing." Privacy & Security Consumer Information, 2007. http://www.informatics.indiana.edu/markus/papers/aci.pdf.

1990s. Originally, AOL would give out free trial memberships that one could use for months with a user supplied a valid credit card number. Many people used algorithmically generated credit card numbers to create accounts for themselves. In 1995, AOL fixed the problem, indirectly creating a new problem - account takeover via phishing.[54] Phishing became so prevalent on the company's systems that they added a disclaimer on all instant messages stating that no employee of AOL will ever ask for your password or billing information. AOL eventually put security controls in place to force the phishers elsewhere.

The next stop for the phishers was the online payment systems and financials. The first direct attempt against a payment system was in June, 2001. The target was e-gold. Although largely viewed as a complete failure, the attack is an example of the cyber criminals evolving their techniques over time. By 2003, phishing had become a global problem and tool kits started to flood the underground.

Since phishing has been around so long, you would think people would become savvy to these types of attacks. Unfortunately, that is not the case. In April, 2004, Gartner Inc, a technology research group, estimated that over 1.78 million Americans succumbed to phishing, giving their information

---

54. Word Spy. "phishing." Word Spy. http://www.wordspy.com.

to cyber criminals. Gartner's most recent estimate of losses to American consumers and the industry is approximately $2.4 billion dollars. A current estimate for phishing puts the consumer response rate at between 1% and 5%. While your firm may like to believe that your users are more technically savvy, they aren't. If a phishing attack blankets some portion of your population, from 1% to 5% of the recipients' will be deceived and their credentials compromised.

If you are the victim of spear phishing, where your users are specifically targeted by name, take action immediately to reduce the risk to your firm. This action may mean going through the painful process of expiring your customers' passwords and requesting they select a new one. If this seems like extreme action, consider the size of your customer base. If you have 1 million customer accounts, a minimally successful attack with a 1% response rate will net the phisher 10,000 accounts. If you are averaging a $5,000 loss per account, you are looking at a risk of $50 million dollars. A well-executed attack, with a 5% rate, could create $250 million dollars in exposure. Remember also, that the total loss per account is not only the loss your firm takes, but the cost of answering the phone when your customer calls in, the salaries you pay your fraud team, the cost of your fraud monitoring systems, and the damage to your brand among other factors. Five thousand dollars in loss per account is a very conservative lower bound to start with.

A recent study showed that less than one percent of all email messages are phishing attacks. Although this number is relatively small, the survey also discovered that each day phishing attacks on the Internet are delivered by a different set of 1000 bots, and 70% of those bots were used to send spam while the remaining 30% were used to proxy back to the web servers. The study also determined that fewer than five bot networks were responsible for all Internet phishing attacks worldwide.[55]

It should be noted for purposes of this book that phishing is currently more of an issue for banks than for brokers. One theory on why this imbalance exists is that the cyber criminals targeting banks are looking to move cash quickly and directly. This strategy often fails with online brokers since strong outbound cash flow controls and the lack of bill payment make extracting the cash a slower process. With that being said, cyber criminals attacking brokerage houses rely on pump-and-dump attacks which take some time to set up and execute. Often, phishing sites are detected and taken down the same day, making them ineffective for use in a pump-and-dump attack. As the speed and effectiveness of the cyber criminal improves, the brokerage industry should see this imbalance evaporate.

55. Cipher Trust. "CipherTrust Proves Worldwide Phishing Attacks Originate from Fewer Than Five Zombie Network Operators." Cipher Trust . www.ciphertrust.com. (accessed September 11, 2007).

Today, there are over 400 free phishing tool kits in the wild, not to mention the professional tool kits.[56] We are now going to explore a professionally built phishing kit known as Rockphish, which as of June 2007, was estimated to be the origin-point for 50% of all phishing spam on the Internet. The cyber criminal often takes an email from the target and reworks it to instill a sense of urgency. Often there is a link that appears to be legitimate but points to a cyber criminal controlled server. The cyber criminals redirect the user to a duplicate of the target's web site in an attempt to get credentials. Often they simply collect the credentials and tell the user that he was incorrect and redirect him to the actual web site of the target. The user reenters his credentials without ever realizing that he has just lost his account information.

Tools & Tips: Look at referrers to your website to see where your users are coming from. With the exception of advertisers or search engines, your users should be hitting your site directly, not via a referrer. Investigate all referrers outside of the norm for possible phishing. Another telltale sign of a phisher is an IP address that is pulling your images down but ignoring content. Often phishers don't go through the trouble of copying the entire site, but simply reference your pictures from their site.

---

56. Mayee Corpin, "Hundreds of Phish Kits on the Loose," Trend Micro blog, May 5, 2008, http://blog.trendmicro.com/over?400?phish?kits?on?the?loose/

Inside Rockphish

Rockphish is one of the most prevalent and successful phishing tool kits on the Internet today. It is necessary to understand Rockphish before you can figure out how to combat it, and phishing in general. This section is an overview of Rockphish. For more detail about phishing, there are some excellent books that cover the topic in great detail.

Once Rockphish compromises a computer, it sets up a proxy that relays requests to a centralized back-end web server. Typically, the server is hosted by an Internet company that offers bullet-proof hosting. A bullet-proof web host guarantees that they will not take the site down no matter what the circumstances are, including requests by law enforcement. You may hear references to hosting firms such as the Russian Business Network, a well known bullet-proof hosting company whose clients are questionable at best. As you can imagine, these servers are often located in countries that have weak or non-existent laws against this type of activity.

Once the back-end web server is in place, it is typically loaded with a large number of fake financial services web sites posing as brokers, banks and the like. Due to this unique configuration, all of the fake financial services web sites are available to all the Rockphish clients. The cyber criminal will then start with the purchase of several very short domain names, such as xyz.com. A recent popular tactic is to use domains in countries where anti-phishing laws are lax and anti-phishing groups don't have contacts, making the phisher that much harder to fight. The phisher will then send out a number of spam emails that contain a spoofed link that actually takes the user to a very long URL. For example:

http://www.bank.com.sessionid123.xyz.com/r1

The first part of the URL appears to be a legitimate financial services site, and it is intended to trick the user. The cyber criminal often uses as much of a legitimate link as he can before he inserts his domain. Through the use of wildcard DNS, the cyber criminal can resolve every subdomain that is sent to his system. In addition, the cyber criminal will often rotate part of the URL to trip up spam filters, or fool honeypots run by various organizations looking for duplicate messages to report as a spam. Rotating the URL also causes problems for systems that rely on URI (links) to determine if a message is spam or a phish. So in the example above, the phisher might continuously rotate the fake session id with every email message.

Since the cyber criminals have so much control over the URL, and can resolve anything sent to them, they can tag their messages to better understand how effective a particular email was. Just like a large marketing firm, they can target different messages to different end users and then determine the most effective URLs! This is just another bit of evidence of the maturity of the criminal enterprise.

The financial services site you reach is solely determined by the first part of the URL. Over the past few months, the Rockphish group has evolved their code to bypass controls put in place to detect them. Originally, the group placed all their files into a directory called rock, which is where their name is derived. In later releases they chose the shorter r1, and now the current vr directory. At some point in the future the directory name will move to something more random in order to bypass some trivial detection schemes implemented by corporate America. Since this group has such a unique method, it has been easy to track the evolution of their code. Initially, the group preferred sending email spam with a section of random text, often derived from online books, followed by a GIF image containing the true message to the user. At one point in time, the Rockphish group was credited for sending approximately half of all the spam worldwide. In addition, the group has claimed that they have stolen in excess of $100 million dollars in 2005 and 2006, and hosted in over 35,000 phishing URLs.[57] Fortunately, once companies could readily identify Rockphish attacks, and take down services became

57. McMillan, Robert. "'Rock Phish' blamed for surge inPhishing." InfoWorld, December 12, 2006. http://www.infoworld.com/article/06/12/12/HNrockphish_1.html

versed in the tool, they have been able to fight back and prevent the uncontrolled growth of attacks.

When a company identifies a phishing site, they initiate a take down of the site via one of the many companies that provide that service. Rockphish sites, however, share their hosts. Once they detect the removal of one, they will automatically switch to any working machine still hosting the site. This robust design presents an extreme challenge to the take down service. In addition the backend systems of Rockphish are often hosted on large servers commonly referred to as mother ships. These mother ships are frequently out of reach of law enforcement, often in countries with corrupt enforcement agencies willing to ignore the activities. Between April 2006 and December 2006, the Russian Business Network (RBN) appeared to be a mother ship for Rockphish. These servers are located in St. Petersburg, Russia and it is extremely difficult to persuade local enforcement or ISPs to take action. RBN has been involved with everything from malware to child pornography. At the time it was a mother ship, it was composed of at least 3 large content servers, hosting up to dozens of fake financial services sites. RBN itself recently disbanded their servers in 2007, and split their operations up. At least a portion of their clients have moved to another bullet-proof hosting company called Abdulla Hosting.

In February 2007, the Rockphish group once again updated its architecture and had it running in limited trials. By March 2007, the new architecture was widely deployed. The architecture works similarly to the old one, but with some improvements. The system would now resolve DNS to five unique IP addresses for a short period, which varied in implementations. Once the time limit had expired it would switch to a new set of five addresses. While this new method "burned' many IP addresses in any given time frame, it did make takedown nearly impossible. The Rockphish group is likely to have a very large bot net, and while a large number of IP addresses may be "burned" for phishing, they can be repurposed for sending out phishing spam.

The group also changed how the code would select a target site on the back end. Initial versions embedded the target site in the URL, which then morphed into inserting the selection information into the HTTP host header. This change further complicates the takedown and tracking of these sites since it makes it more difficult to tell which sites are live and which ones aren't.

A proper phish may not need to use a bogus domain if there are minor flaws on your web server. One phishing method allows the user to hit the actual financial web site in a frame and then lift the credentials out without causing any cross-site script issues. An attack like this is very difficult for the average user to detect since they are technically at the correct site, albeit within a frame.[58] With some additional code on your web server, however, you can easily defeat this attack.

Your website should always be configured, at minimum, to prevent the login box of your site from breaking out of its frame via JavaScript or other methods. Always check, and warn your user if a non-framed page is detected running in a frame. Login pages should also check the referrer to validate that the user is not connecting to you via an unexpected method.

Another interesting, relatively recent phish involves using the client's home router against them. Most users don't change their very-well-known default passwords. These users also likely don't update the firmware on their routers, leaving potential exploits open. The attack against the router installs some malicious code that alters where specified domains resolve to, so even though your client entered the correct URL you are redirected to the cyber criminal's site. Even if your client uses a stored favorite, they are automatically redirected to a malicious site.

---

58. Mikx Browser Security Research blog, "Alpha Phising [IE 6 WinXP SP2]," comment posted September 8, 2004, http://www.mikx.de/index.php?p=2.

Combating Phishing

There are four main methods for combating phishing. While other methods exist, the following are the most widely used.

Educating Your Customer

The first method involves training users to recognize the phish. Initially, results with this approach were very promising. Like most cyber attacks, phishing attacks have became more complex and more realistic, mimicking the target site exactly, pulling in more and more victims. In 2004 a study was performed at West Point Military Academy. The student body is informed, educated, and computer savvy. Unfortunately the results were horrible. Over 80% of the 500 users fell for the phish and revealed personal information.[59] User education alone is not the solution.

Some companies have attempted to mitigate the problem of phishing sites by altering the images on their site if they are retrieved in a non-standard way. Typically the company's logo is stamped with a message to the user stating that the site is fraudulent. Of course, criminals defeat this method by simply replicating the entire site down to the images.[60]

59. Bank, David. "Spear Phishing' Test Educate People About Online Scams." The Wall Street Journal , Aug 17, 2005.

Tools & Tips: Never, ever send a URL to your
users. Clearly state to your users that you will
never, ever send them a URL via email. Companies are currently moving to secure inboxes
to avoid phishing. Phishers have simply
phished the secure inbox with messages saying
"You have an important email at company A,
please click the link below to retrieve it from
you secure inbox" defeating most companies
implementation of these systems.

Additionally, you should augment your mail
systems with simple authentication systems such
as Sender Policy Framework (SPF) to reduce the
chance of emails being spoofed. While this system
isn't wide spread it is catching on.

The Blacklist

The second method is to maintain a list of
known bad sites, the phishing web pages, and
check all links for membership on that list. Most of
the latest versions of web browsers contain various
levels of anti-phishing technology, including
Microsoft Internet Explorer 7.0, Mozilla Firefox 2.0
and Opera 9.1. Firefox is currently utilizing blacklists from Google, a combination of lists from various sources. Opera is utilizing blacklists from the
PhishTank and GeoTrust. As you can imagine, the
use of the blacklist technique brings up several

---

60. Krebs, Brian. "Using Images to Fight Phishing." Wall Street Journal,
Security Fix section, August 31, 2006.

issues. First there is a major privacy issue, since every time you surf to a website it is checked against a master list. It would be quite easy for the anti-phishing company to track your IP and every site you visit. The second major issue is that the effectiveness is roughly the same as an anti-virus vendor; it is not a proactive, but a reactive service. Once a phish is reported or detected, it will be added to a list which must propagate. Propagation takes time. If a phish is properly targeted, and not blindly mailed to millions of users, it could be days or weeks before detection. The third issue is that these anti-phishing sites could be used for denial of service if they have no permanent white list feature. A cyber criminal could report your domain many times, using hundreds of thousands of different IP addresses, (Remember BOT networks?), confusing your users by stating that they are on a phishing site, not your actual web site. Often, it takes up to twenty four hours to get off these lists due to replication and caching.

Tools & Tips: A better method to validate a phishing site would be to use white lists with IPs and some intelligent fingerprinting. Caution must be taken, however, as some sort of proxy or middle-man could respond to validation requests, and thereby defeat the system.

Two-Factor

The third major method is the augmentation of
security with a personal image on any password
page. The site instructs users not to enter their
passwords unless they see their personal image. A
recent study suggests that users largely ignore
these types of security controls.[61] This result is
unsurprising, as there already was a two-way SSL
authentication in place. Granted, looking at a picture is easier than validating an SSL certificate.
The picture, however, removes all the important
security indicators that an SSL certificate has.
Studies have shown that users largely ignore when
a site goes from being secured by SSL to being
unsecured, indicating that your average user
doesn't even look for the little lock icon at the bottom of the browser. Like all two-factor authentication systems, personal image systems can succumb
to man-in-the-middle attacks. Nordea, a Scandina-
vian bank, in 2005,[62] and Citibank, in 2006, [63] were
both targets of large scale of attacks of this nature.

61. Schechter, Stuart, Dhamija, Rachna, Ozment, Andy, and Fischer, Ian,
"The Emperor's New Security Indicators: An evaluation of website
authentication and the effect of role playing on usability studies,"
IEEE Symposium on Security and Privacy, Oakland, CA, May 2007.

62. Finextra. "Phishers target Nordea's one?time password system." Finextra, (Oct. 12, 2005), http://www.finextra.com/fullstory.asp?id=14384.

63. Krebs, Brian. "Citibank Phish Spoofs 2?Factor Authentication." Wall
Street Journal, Security Fix section, July 10, 2006. http://blog.washing-
tonpost.com/securityfix/2006/07/
citibank_phish_spoofs_2factor_1.html.

Some suggest that dynamic security skins[64] might be the next step in using images as a two-way authentication scheme. The idea is to overlay a user-selected image across the login form, indicating that the form is legitimate. These images are shared between the user and the browser instead of the user and the website. The system relies on a mutual authentication protocol, making it less vulnerable to attack than other systems. Although this step is headed in the right direction, recent studies question whether the user will even pay attention to the picture. Dynamic security skins also require a trusted browser. If you already have a trusted browser, dynamic security skins become irrelevant, as site validation could be built into the browser itself.

Identification and Takedown

The fourth and final method of phish fighting is categorized as identification and takedown. There are several companies that continuously monitor the Internet to detect, analyze and assist in shutting down phishing websites.[65] Do your homework when shopping these services; do not just look at the mean time to takedown. Some companies can actually retrieve credentials, passwords, and other PII from phishing sites prior to

64. Dhamija, Rachna, and Tygar, J.D., "The Battle Against Phishing: Dynamic Security Skins," Symposium On Usable Privacy and Security (SOUPS), Pittsburgh, PA, 2005.

65. Anti-Phishing Working Group. http://www.antiphishing.org.

takedown, demonstrating which users have been compromised. This service allows you to take proactive steps, such as locking accounts, informing customers and most importantly, changing the users' credentials.

Tools & Tips: Your site must have an easy method for users to report phishing attempts. Wherever you decide to place the link, both customers and non-customers should be able to locate it quickly. Clearly explain all the information required to report the phish and how to obtain it. For example, you might request email headers and contents of the email message. Outside users are often the first to provide information as they quickly realize that they do not do business with you. Customers don't report as quickly, since they just assume it's another piece of junk mail.

Terms

Bullet Proof Hosting – A service provider that takes a no-questions-asked approach to the materials they place on their site. They typically guarantee that they will never take a site down even when pressured by law enforcement. This flexibility comes at a substantial price over conventional hosters. Most bullet proof hosts are in China, South America, parts of Asia and Russia.

DNS – Domain Name System. DNS is a system that allows for the translation of domain names into IP addresses. Typically in the form of host.domain.tld.

GIF – Graphics Interchange Format. A GIF is a popular graphics format that was introduced by CompuServe in 1987.

Headers – In email, they are a block of data that appear at the top of the message, typically hidden from the user by most email clients. The headers identify the sender and recipient, along with the route the email message took. Unfortunately, headers can be faked and cannot be relied upon as factual.

Honeypot – A system, file or other object whose goal it is to attract cyber criminals.

HTTP Host Header – Host headers allow you to setup multiple domains on one single IP address.

Man-In-The-Middle - A man-in-the-middle is when the attacker makes independent connections with the victim and the destination. This allows the attacker to eavesdrop on the conversation between the two systems.

Mother ship – A centralized large server that hosts content, typically accessed via proxy systems

URI – Uniform Resource Identifier, a short compact string of characters used to identify a network resource.

URL - Universal Resource Locator, a synonym for URI.

Wildcard DNS – A domain that is configured to resolve any host at the domain e.g. anything.domain.tld

CHAPTER 10 # Inside a Trojan

There is only one admirable form of the imagination: the imagination that is so intense that it creates a new reality, that it makes things happen.

- Sean O'Faolain

This chapter comes with a warning. We are going to look at one popular trojan that targets financial service companies. Trojans, while easy to explain, are very complex applications. Any discussion about them quickly turns into a discussion involving technical jargon. While this author made every attempt to keep this chapter non-technical, I simply can't be held responsible for your brain exploding by the end of the chapter.

An Overview of PRG (Windows Only)

PRG, also commonly referred to as NTOS after the name of the core executable in this trojan, is a particularly nasty piece of malware. PRG has been gaining favor with cyber criminals ever since the authors of the popular HaxDoor decided to stop evolving their code, effectively taking it off the market.

PRG hijacks specific processes running on your computer. Once the malware injects a process, all PRG activities appear to be coming from the hijacked process. This technique was discussed way back in chapter 6 when we talked about Windows APIs and hooks into other processes. Some Microsoft Windows processes, such as Internet Explorer, communicate with the outside world, and they are allowed through the local firewall without user prompting. By crafting a trojan that can piggyback one of these processes, the trojan evades the firewall and detection by the end user.

What makes PRG particularly painful is that it injects code into a library that is used by a number of Internet functions. By injecting into this particular library, the trojan is able to read any request made by the user. By tapping into the operating system at this point, PRG circumvents any encryption between the browser and the website, such as SSL.

Since the author of this book completed this technical analysis of PRG, the trojan has built on prior versions and morphed into a more dangerous form. At least one new variation is used specifically to target banking clients with commercial banking accounts. The latest trojan sends an alert to the cyber criminal when the victim logs into his banking account. This alert allows the attacker to bypass any front-end authentication schemes such as enhanced authentication, smart cards, tokens, etc. Once PRG has communicated back to the cyber criminal's server, it notifies the backend servers which bank the victim uses. The command and control server then automatically feeds bank-specific scripts back to the trojan. The commands tell the trojan how to simulate transactions for that bank, including information on screen navigation and instructions for performing transactions such as ACH and wire transfers. The trojan also simulates keystrokes to avoid various anti-fraud systems. Due to the innovative use of transaction simulating scripts, a cyber criminal can stay one step ahead of the institution without having to update the trojan.[66] In addition, authentication controls the financial institution may have in place become permanently irrelevant.

PRG is now capable of circumventing most enhanced authentication systems in place or on the drawing board.

Technical Analysis of PRG/NTOS

Unfortunately, the analysis of trojans is both complex and slow, bordering more on an art form than anything else. This section is provided for those who are technically savvy and wish to know more about the inner workings of a trojan. Alternatively, this section is for those having trouble sleeping and in need of a riveting trojan analysis/ soporific. The analysis contained in this section is from a sample of PRG acquired by this author around June 2007. Due to the speed at which these systems mutate, by the time analysis was complete it was already obsolete.

To infect your systems, the PRG executable injects itself into the Winlogon process of the system. The Winlogon process appears in most versions of the Microsoft Windows operating system and is normally responsible for login functions,

66. Jackson, Don. "Hackers Use Stealthy, New Prg Banking Trojan to Attack Commercial Banking Clients in Four Countries." Secure Works.
http://www.secureworks.com/research/threats/bankingprg/ ?threat=bankingprg.

such as profile loading and locking the screen saver. Once Winlogon is injected, the process spawns two additional threads. The first thread executes inside svchost.exe, while the second thread creates a named pipe server for communication with other running threads.

The injected svchost.exe process is the work horse in this piece of malware. The scvhost.exe process is a generic process, on all Windows computer systems, designed to group together services that run from dynamic-link libraries. Its broad reach makes svchost.exe very useful for executing malicious code. Few users ever question this process. The code running from svchost.exe is responsible for injecting a thread into all the active processes on the computer system, with a few exceptions. It skips its own process, the system idle process, and Csrss.exe. It skips Csrss.exe because it is a critical process within the operating system, and very difficult to inject without causing severe system problems. Nearly all other processes are targeted. PRG then goes on to create three new threads responsible for downloading new code, passing data to the cyber criminal's web server, and sending status information to the cyber criminals for statistical and control purposes.

The most important part of this malware, the part responsible for grabbing the user's personal information, are the hooks that look at the HttpSendRequestA(), HttpSendRequestW(), HttpSendRequestExA() and HttpSendRequestExW() functions from the wininet.dll on the computer. For those of you unfamiliar with the wininet.dll, this dynamic-link library contains a number of program components for various Internet related functions, including FTP, Gopher and HTTP. The major benefit of hooking wininet.dll is that it allows PRG to inspect any program that uses Windows API functions. Once hooks are placed into this component, the cyber criminal can read and steal any data in the request buffer.

The earlier implementations of PRG only stole POST requests with the content-type application/x-www-form-urlencoded. In later releases PRG started to log keystrokes directly. Instead of looking for post data, it also stole FTP user ids, passwords, and clipboard data. PRG also appeared to gain the ability to take screen shots of the infected computer. The malware also grabs the system's IP address, system time, operating system version, revision and build numbers, default language, and a few other data points. To make the takeover permanent and irreversible, later versions of PRG also put backdoors into the target system.

Tools & Tips: Most authors of malware tend to hook API functions rather than every program on the victim's computer. API functions have a common interface that allows an author to write one piece of code to interpret any data that uses the API. A potential workaround would be to build a fat client, or perhaps an ActiveX control, that runs within the browser that terminates the HTTPS traffic on its own, rather than utilizing the Windows API. Even with this solution, it would still only be a matter of time before the cyber criminals adapted. This method would also require additional protections to prevent the process from being hooked, or at least detecting if it has been hooked. Counter-measures of this sort will always be at risk for a blue screen of death (BSOD), etc.

Once fully installed, PRG compares the data that it has captured to a list of criteria. When it finds a match, it encrypts the data to disk. Svchost.exe picks up the encrypted data and sends it to the cyber criminal's web site of choice. By encrypting data and sending it off asynchronously, this malware thwarts many pieces of anti-trojan software that look for the movement of your credentials. In addition, the delay could circumvent behavior based anti-trojan software.

Fortunately, unlike many pieces of malware, PRG does little to protect itself from detection. It also has some interesting flaws that will likely be repaired in future releases. We'll go into more detail on those flaws later. PRG uses only a single technique to evade protection-type services running on the computer. Another section of code uses only a single technique to bypass detection by signature-based systems. Based on the code, there is no reason the authors of this malware could not or would not utilize more complex stealth routines in future releases. Even with this minimalist approach to stealth, this PRG does have some tricks up its virtual sleeve.

Upon launching, PRG enumerates processes to determine if there are any potentially threatening protection services running. Simultaneously, it copies itself to disk and sets the registry to run it at startup. If any of the enumerated processes look like trouble, PRG terminates itself instead of injecting any of the processes.

Up until this point, most malware writers would just attempt to use an aggressive approach on the protective processes in an attempt to successfully inject. Unfortunately, aggressive attacks often suddenly remove an icon from the system tray or trigger a pop-up notification. Because PRG simply terminates when it sees one of these tools running, it goes completely undetected. Upon the next reboot, PRG will start and inject processes before any protection software has started, going completely undetected. Much like in life, patience is a virtue, even in malware.

PRG evades signature based systems by using an extremely basic system, one almost as simplistic as the process checking function. When the trojan copies itself to the local computer, it uses the Copy-File() function from the Kernel32 library to create the exe. Once this file has been created, it sets the file pointer to the end of the file and appends random data to the file. This data is never referenced by the code later. Clearly it is an attempt to bypass any anti-virus or anti-trojan system that works by hashing files, or by checking the end of files for part of their signatures.

While PRG so far has seemed pretty simplistic, it's actually quite effective. Like everything, though, PRG is not without its flaws. We will go into some detail around them. While the coders obviously have a professional level of skill, you can see that there are some gaps in their knowledge or moments of laziness where they use code that they believe is "good enough". We will go in increasing order of difficult in fixing these flaws. If fixed, PRG could go from being an annoyance to the bane of your organization. If you wanted to escape the technical section, this is your last chance.

Flaws in PRG/NTOS

This section made its way into the chapter to show you that much like commercial software; malware does not have to be bug free to be successful. With most end users running incorrectly secured machines, the bar is much lower for malware writers.

In the analyzed version of PRG, there is a flaw in the protection process checking function. The process checking routine only looks for a process called outpost.exe, the process for the Outpost Pro Firewall. PRG uses this section to determine if it should load immediately, or shut down and wait for a reboot. Several conclusions can be drawn from this weird section of code. First, the author may charge for additional stealth capabilities. To achieve a lower profile, he simply has to add additional information to the array and recompile the code. Second, he is anticipating additional capabilities and signatures may be added to various products. When that occurs he simply updates a section of his program, morphing the code. Third, for some reason the Outpost Pro Firewall detects PRG. This last option seems unlikely, although the author of this book did not have time to verify this possibility. Fourth, there may be another piece of malware in the wild that has the name of outpost.exe that causes issues with PRG. There is no evidence currently to support this incompatibility argument. The author of PRG will likely consider adding in the most popular anti-virus, anti-trojan, anti-spyware software along with the most popular all-in-one packages to minimize detection. There are a few trojans today that are aware of over 700 security software packages. Adding in a fairly comprehensive list is at most a few minutes of work.

PRG uses static names and locations for most files - a huge security no-no. Consistent file names and directories make it easy to detect a given piece of malware, even if the trojan uses other forms of stealth. The main file is usually called ntos.exe, located in the Microsoft Windows system directory. The code also generates a directory under system called wsnpoem, and stores stolen data in a file called audio.dll. Basic configuration data is also stored in this directory in the video.dll file. PRG's registry keys and names are consistent, along with object names. Later releases changed a few file names, but the core files remained unchanged. The PRG author could easily alter the code to change this information to random values for each infection, making static entry detection useless. Another interesting way of hiding would be to simply use the names of unused DLLs on the system.

Later evolutions of PRG opened up back doors to the end user's computer. Open ports are dead giveaways and may immediately alert a user to the infection. This issue may be a function of scope creep, similar to that experienced at large companies. Tools start off with basic features, and soon everything, including the kitchen sink, is thrown in. Continued use of backdoors in this code will certainly make PRG easier to detect, unless the author can add some advanced rootkit technology to hide these ports. But like anything, nothing is truly hidden when you know where to look.

The way PRG sends its captured data to the drop server is also a huge issue. PRG uses a content-type of binary which is strange enough. It then waits for the server response when posting data. Instead of using the standard normal HTTP 200 (OK) status message, it looks for a custom response "HALL: OK" This message lets the malware know that the upload was successful. When it receives confirmation, PRG deletes the local file. These steps can all be used for detection. The first issue is the content-type of binary. An intrusion detection system (IDS) can detect this signature. Even worse, the HALL: OK response is completely unique and easily detectable by any IDS. The future direction of this code would likely be to use common content-types, obfuscate the upload data via GET requests, and encode the data in the call. The HALL: OK response could shift to the standard HTTP 200 (OK) response. In addition, PRG should not immediately delete the local captured data file. Some anti-trojan systems may detect the malware by correlating its actions. PRG's authors could simply add a random time delay before the encrypted file is deleted or simply re-encrypt the data with a random key, which would protect the data from ever being recovered.

PRG is not out of the woods yet. The malware also has a "phone home" function that updates the root server with status information and registers new PRG installations. Although the attacker can change the format of this string, he often doesn't. Below is an example of a phone home. The underlined section is consistent from machine to machine, making it easy to create an IDS or anti-trojan signature that detects this format.

http://192.168.4.1/s.php?2=1&n=2

This hole can be easily fixed by encrypting some of the data and fixing the statement to further reflect a post. The authors could encode the IP data with alpha characters, prefix that data with a random number of alpha characters, and append a common top level domain, such as .com, .net, .org or .edu. In addition, the status data should be encoded also using some similar randomization system. Static pieces are easily crafted into detection signatures.

There are also minor issues with the data captured by PRG. As you may recall, the malware captures POST requests that have the content-type of "application/x-www-form-urlencoded". In addition to stealing that data, it also grabs the IP address, system time, the operating system version, revision and build numbers, default language, and a few other data points of the end user system. The author clearly intended to collect this information for statistics. With an IP address, however, it's possible to launch an attack from a location geographically close to the target machine. This technique bypasses most geolocation systems on the market today, and it may be the tipping point to get beneath a threshold in a rule based risk system. PRG's author unfortunately failed to capture a very important data point, the USER-AGENT and the ACCEPT-LANGUAGE fields in the browser header. With these points it's possible to further impersonate the user by matching the target's browser. While this approach won't necessarily bypass any detection system, it may help to reduce the risk score enough to avoid generating alerts. It would be safe to assume that this data will be available in future releases of the code.

Data encryption is a long standing issue with any trojan that encrypts data. PRG is no different. The malware loops through the data byte by byte and changes the value depending on whether the byte is even or odd in the sequence. Early versions of PRG used the LZNT1 algorithm, available in the ntdll.dll, to compress the data. Later releases use a different algorithm. Fortunately for the virus writers, the algorithm is sufficient to perplex any anti-virus software. PRG also uses this same algorithm to encrypt the destination URLs for the stolen data. Once you can decrypt the destination URLs, you have a good chance of retrieving any stolen data. If that occurs, then the cyber criminal's work was for naught. At some point it's likely that PRG will implement a strong encryption algorithm with a public/private key system, making it impossible to retrieve the data. All the libraries for PKI are typically present on most modern operating systems, and it would be a likely next step by the cyber criminal.

If you are unfamiliar with the concept of public/private key encryption, here's a quick explanation. This type of encryption utilizes a pair of keys that are mathematically related. You use the public key to encrypt your data, and you keep your private key safe. You can distribute your public key anywhere, since it cannot be used to decrypt what has been encrypted. The public key also cannot be used to derive the private key. Only the private key can decrypt the data. Using this method puts the forensic analyst in the spot of having to brute force the private key. Brute force attacks against private keys are often computationally infeasible. The only other path is to exploit a flaw in the implementation of the encryption algorithm to decrypt the data.

There is also a minor flaw the way the code injects. PRG uses the CreateRemoteThread() function, as discussed earlier in this book, to inject itself. While the actual issue is out of the scope of this book, the flaw revolves around the VirtualAllocEX() function for the remote process. The author of PRG appears to be lazy. If the region of memory has been committed when the VirtualAllocEx() function is called, it simply fails and the code hook never occurs, an obvious flaw. Perhaps the author didn't quite understand how to rebase PRG's base address in a remote process. The author did manage to rebase his own image elsewhere in the code, so this coding error will likely be fixed in a future release.

PRG uses a rather simplistic method to circumvent anti-virus systems. While it's possible that the original intent of the random characters added to the end of the file was to circumvent hash checking, the author should be more concerned with anti-virus software. Anti-virus systems do not check an entire file against the hundreds of thousands of patterns that are stored in the pattern files. To avoid affecting system performance, most anti-virus vendors check only a portion of the file. Some check the first kilobyte of a file. Others check the last couple of kilobytes of a file. Still others will use an algorithm to sample pieces of the file. Since these techniques are so wide spread in the industry, it's quite easy to bypass these types of checks.

The author of PRG could easily incorporate a basic morphing system that could inject nonsense code into random spots in the malware. Simply inserting no operation (NOP) statements, setting dummy variables to random values, or inserting other non-functional dummy code could be enough to confuse most anti-virus systems, making it difficult if not impossible to build an accurate pattern for the virus. As long as these inserts occurred frequently in the head and tail of the code, PRG could be very difficult to detect.

The last major issue with PRG is not a flaw with the malware itself. Intrusion detection systems can detect the encoded URL string in the Microsoft DOS header. Even though the malware is properly packed with the ultimate packer for executables, known as UPX, an intrusion detection system can detect the malware because UPX does not alter the Microsoft DOS headers. To avoid detection by systems that can read this header, the authors must fix this issue.

This chapter took you through the inside of one piece of malware. It shows that no matter how good someone thinks his code is, there are always faults within it. These faults, along with greed for more compromised credentials, are what drive the continuous evolution between the good guys and the cyber criminals.

Again, the author apologizes for all the tech jargon contained in this chapter. If you made it through the entire chapter, you're in good shape.

Terms

Accept-Language – A text string sent to the web
server during a request by the browser
that tells the web server the preferred
response language of the web page.

BSOD – Blue Screen of Death. A BSOD, also
known as a stop error, is a screen displayed on certain operating systems that
occurs when a critical system error is
encountered. This causes the operating
system to shut down to prevent damage.

FTP – File Transfer Protocol. FTP is a protocol
used to transfer data between two computers on a network.

Gopher- A network protocol designed for the
Internet for the purpose of distributed
document search and retrieval.

IDS – Intrusion Detection System. IDS is a
piece of software that detects attacks on
computer systems.

Microsoft DOS Header – A block of data at the
start of an EXE file that defines various
parameters of the file.

Packer – A computer program designed to compress another program to reduce its size or obfuscate the underlying code.

PKI – Public Key Infrastructure. A general term for the required software for using asymmetric encryption.

Post – A method in HTTP that submits data.

Signature – A subset of features taken to reduce the amount of comparison work to validate a match. It is sometimes also referred to as a fingerprint.

SSL – Secure Sockets Layer. SSL is a set of cryptographic protocols that provides secure communications between two computers.

Threads – A part of a computer program that can execute independently of the other parts.

UPX – Ultimate Packer for Executables. UPX is an open-source compression algorithm.

User-Agent – A text string sent to the web server by the browser that includes information such as application name, version, host operating system and language.

CHAPTER 11 Distribution Systems

The whole problem with the world is that fools and fanatics are always so certain of themselves, but wiser people so full of doubts.

- Bertrand Russell

The jack-of-all-trades cyber criminal has essentially disappeared, likely due to the fact that both
sides have become increasingly skilled. As you
saw in the last chapter, malware and trojans have
evolved into sharpened tools. Rootkit writing is
not the same thing as exploiting an operating system. A sophisticated piece of code needs an
equally sophisticated distribution system. The
goal of the attacker is to stay under the anti-virus
radar as long as possible. To do that, the cyber
criminal often turns to a group that specializes in
the distribution of malware.

MPack Overview

MPack was proof of concept code around June
2006. By August of that year it became a commercial product. In October 2006 it was being sold
mainly in Russian forums. It has since received
several updates, and still has room to add additional exploits. The authors of the MPack are currently claiming up to a fifty percent infection rate.
As of this writing, on public source credits it with
ten percent of web based exploits.[67]

The MPack tool was written by the "Dream
Coders" team, a group of three criminal hackers.
DCT, Fuzka and an unidentified third member

67. LeClaire, Jennifer. "Security Experts Monitor MPack Threat." News-
factor.com, June 21, 2007. http://www.newsfactor.com/news/Security-
Experts-Monitor-MPack-Threat/story.xhtml?story_id=020000202THK.

compose "Dream Coders". Many groups refer to a fourth person, a cyber criminal by the name of $ash, also known as SaSH, Alex and Alexxx. While $ash claims to be a member of Dream Coders, and is talented programmer in his own right, his role is more of a marketing person for that group. $ash also appears linked to the BlackLogic group. Dream Coders may also be linked to BlackLogic.

There are roughly 108 active users on the Blacklogic.net web site. The most active users are parasite, KCEOH, 500mhz and admin. This site hosts a variety of tool kits and how-to guides. Participants on the Blacklogic forums appear to be writing their own code as a group. They are also exchanging ideas and helping with beta testing of new code. To give you an idea of how skilled this group is, in late December of 2005 the group was focused on a project to read the content of the Windows 2000 System Table supporting native API calls. This code requires extremely advanced knowledge of the operating system architecture along with access to a large number of undocumented operating system API calls, or access to internal Microsoft documentation on the subject. This group is credited with Backdoor.Sdbot, along with other pieces of malware.

The Dream Coders do get occasional help from other Russian programmers. They also rely on multiple outside sources for exploits. Typically either an outsider sends in an exploit, or the group receives proof of concept code which they then

massage into a working exploit for MPack. The
group also uses testers from other countries to validate their work. On occasion, they will purchase
exploits for implementation into their product.
Zero-day exploits which are highly prized, can
fetch in excess of $10,000 in the underground.[68]

MPack is sometimes incorrectly referred to as
WebAttack 2. While the authors of MPack know
the WebAttack group, they are separate and distinct products. The WebAttack 2 pack is in the
design phase and should be on the market shortly.

The Italian Job

The last major attack using MPack was known
as the Italian Job, due to the fact the targets were
mostly Italian domains, occurred in June 2007. The
attack involved over 80,000 unique IP addresses. It
is currently believed that the attackers gained
access to these sites via an exploit in cPanel, a popular management tool for users hosting web sites.

How does one infect so many domains? The
cyber criminal first started with a list of stolen or
purchased FTP accounts. They automatically vali-
dated the credentials with a PHP script called
ftp_check.php. The cyber criminals loaded the sto-

---

68. ScanSafe, "Annual Global Threat Report: Trends for January 20007-
December 2007," ScanSafe, San Mateo, CA, 2008.

len account lists into one file, called *acc.txt*, and sorted the valid ones into a file called *valid.txt*.

The criminals took the valid credentials and utilized a vulnerability scanning program such as FTP-Toolz pack, RooT [iFrame] or FTPCheckI-frame. These programs are relatively cheap, as low as $25 each. They look for vulnerable web servers and automatically infect hundreds of thousands of web pages with the MPack IFRAME.

The attack inserts unfriendly iFrame code and redirects unsuspecting web surfers to an exploit page set up by the MPack software on these vulnerable servers. Upon connecting to the unfriendly page, MPack inspects the surfer's HTTP headers to identify the target machine's browser and operating system (OS). The site systematically attempts to find an exploit for that specific browser and OS. When it finds one, it downloads a piece of malware of the attacker's choosing.

Torpig is a frequently chosen piece of malware. In the last attack with MPack, the Torpig code tied back to the Russian Business Network (RBN), discussed in an earlier chapter.

Technical Analysis of MPACK

At the time of this writing, MPACK was on version 0.94. It has been growing rapidly and new capabilities are likely in place since this analysis was completed. MPACK is currently sold in a Russian forum for around $1000, with an add-on module, DreamDownloader, for an additional $300. DreamDownloader is a relatively new module that simplifies the attack process for the cyber criminal. All the cyber criminal needs to do now is specify the URL of the malicious code file they want to download. DreamDownloader creates an executable file and carries out the process. The resulting executable is advertised as capable of bypassing multiple firewalls and disabling some anti-virus programs. MPACK protects itself by using anti-debugger techniques. It can detect if it is executing in a virtual computer, and it can be packed using several compression systems including Upack, UPX or Mew.

With the purchase of MPack, you receive one year worth of support. It also includes a guarantee that it will not be detected by any anti-virus system. Product updates are not included, but you can obtain new exploits for between $50 and $150 depending on the complexity and rarity of the exploit. Currently the code includes ten exploits, six being Microsoft Windows or Internet Explorer exploits.

The exploit list contained in MPack now includes:

Exploit Name: Microsoft Windows Animated Cursor Buffer Overflow

CVE Reference: CVE-2007-0038

Impacts: Windows 2000 SP4 to Vista with Internet Explorer 6 & 7

Description: There is a stack buffer overflow in the code used by Microsoft Windows to load and process animated cursor files. Microsoft Windows does not properly check the size of the animated cursor file header within animated cursor files, leading to the exploit.

How the attacker uses this: This exploit impacts both Microsoft Explorer 6 and 7 and allows the attacker to infect the target computer without any user interaction. Upon successfully executing the exploit, the attacker would have complete control over the victim's computer.

Exploit Name: Vulnerability in the Microsoft Data Access Components

CVE Reference: CVE-2006-0003

Impacts: Any Windows platform utilizing MDAC 2.5 SP3 to 2.8 SP2

Description: There is a remote code execution vulnerability in the RDS.Dataspace ActiveX control. This control is part of the Microsoft Data Access Components.

How the attacker uses this: This exploit allows the attacker to infect the target computer without any user interaction. Upon successfully executing the exploit, the attacker would have the same rights as the user currently logged into the system.

Exploit Name: Vulnerability in Windows Media Player Plug-in with Non-Microsoft Internet Browsers

CVE Reference: CVE-2006-0005

Impacts: Windows 2000 to XP SP2, including Windows Server 2000 & 2003,

Description: There is a remote code execution vulnerability in the way the Windows Media Player plug-in handles a malformed EMBED element.

How the attacker uses this: An attacker could craft a web site that contains a page with a media player skin. Once on that page, the user would be prompted to download the skin. The download would infect the user's computer. Upon successfully executing the exploit, the attacker would have complete control over the victim's computer.

Exploit Name: Vulnerability in Vector Markup Language (VML)

CVE Reference: CVE-2006-4868

Impacts: Windows 2000 SP4 to XP SP2, including Windows Server 2003 SP1, Outlook 2003 & Internet Explorer 6.0

Description: There is a Stack-based buffer overflow in the Vector Graphics Rendering engine that allows remote attackers to execute arbitrary code.

How the attacker uses this: This exploit allows the attacker to infect the target computer without any user interaction. Upon successfully executing the exploit, the attacker would have complete control over the victim's computer.

Exploit Name: MMC Cross-Site Scripting

CVE Reference: CVE-2006-3643

Impacts: Microsoft Internet Explorer 5.01, and Microsoft Internet Explorer 6.0 with Windows Server 2003 SP1

Description: There is a cross-site scripting vulnerability that allows access to local html embedded resource files in the Microsoft Management Console library.

How the attacker uses this: This exploit requires assistance from the target. An attacker would craft a web site that contains a page that exploits this vulnerability. Once on the page, the user would be prompted to perform several other actions, after which the attack would occur. The attacker could attempt to automate the user responses, making it invisible to the user. Upon successfully executing the exploit, the attacker would have the same rights as the user currently logged into the system.

Exploit Name: XML Core Service Overflow

CVE Reference: CVE-2006-5745

Impacts: Any version of Windows with XML Core Services 4.0 or 6.0

Description: There is a code vulnerability in the setRequestHeader method that is used by the XML HTTP ActiveX control.

How an attacker would use this: This exploit allows the attacker to infect the target computer without any user interaction. Upon successfully executing the exploit, the attacker would have complete control over the victim's computer.

Exploit Name: Shell Remote Code Execution

CVE Reference: CVE-2006-3730

Impacts: Microsoft Internet Explorer 6.0 & 6.0 SP1

Description: There is an integer overflow in the Common Controls library used by Microsoft Windows for various functions.

How an attacker would use this: This exploit allows the attacker to infect the target computer without any user interaction. Upon successfully executing the exploit, the attacker would have the same rights as the user currently logged into the system.

Exploit Name: WinZip ActiveX Overflow

CVE Reference: CVE-2006-3890

Impacts: WinZip 7.0-10.0 or any software utilizing the Sky Software FileView ActiveX Control

Description: There is a stack buffer overflow in the FileView ActiveX control used in WinZip 10 and some other applications.

How an attacker would use this: An attacker would craft a web site that contains a page with a specially crafted image file to exploit this vulnerability. Once on the page, the infection, which due to the nature of the flaw would have approximately a 17% success rate, would occur without any user interaction. Upon successfully executing the exploit, the attacker would have complete control over the victim's computer.

Exploit Name: QuickTime Overflow

CVE Reference: CVE-2007-0714

Impacts: Apple Quicktime 5.0 to 7.1.4

Description: There is an integer overflow in Apple QuickTime that allows an attacker to execute arbitrary code via a crafted QuickTime movie.

How an attacker would use this: An attacker would craft a web site that contains a page with a specially crafted QuickTime file to exploit this vulnerability. This exploit allows the attacker to infect the target computer without any user inter-action. Upon successfully executing the exploit, the attacker would have complete control over the victim's computer.

Exploit Name: GDI Rendering Engine

CVE Reference: CVE-2006-5758

Impacts: Microsoft Windows 2000 SP4 to Micro-soft Windows XP SP2

Description: The Graphics Rendering Engine (GDI) maps data to a read-only shared memory section that another process can remap, making it read-write.

How an attacker would use this: This exploit allows the attacker to infect the target computer without any user interaction. Upon successfully executing the exploit, the attacker would have complete control over the victim's computer.

For additional information on these exploits, look up the details at the NIST CVE web site or contact the owners of the individual components.

This chapter has exposed just one tool the cyber criminals have at their disposal to infect your clients. These tools are constantly evolving, with new ones appearing all the time. For example, Pushdo and Tornado are new threats that should be gaining their share of press shortly.[69,70]

69. Stewart, Joe. "Pushdo – Analysis of a Modern Malware Distribution System." Security Works. http://www.securityworks.com/reasearch/threats/pushdo/.

70. Nichols, Shaun. "Experts warn of 'Tornado' hacker tool." Vnunet.com.
http://www.vnunet.com/vnunet/news/2214938/web?attack?tool?discovered.

Terms

Buffer – A region of memory used to temporarily hold input or output data.

Command-line – An all text display where commands can be entered.

cPanel – Control Panel. cPanel is a popular graphical, web-based interface designed to simplify the administration of a website.

iFrame – Inline frame. An iFrame allows you to embed another HTML document inside of the main document.

NIST - National Institute of Science and Technology. NIST is a government agency that develops and promotes measurements.

PHP – Hypertext Preprocessor. PHP is a programming language that allows for the creation of dynamic content that interfaces with databases.

Torpig – Torpig is a trojan horse that targets Microsoft Windows machines. Torpig turns off anti-virus applications, installs remote access capabilities, steals user credentials, modifies files and attempts to install additional malware on the computer.

Zero-Day Exploits – A vulnerability in a piece of software that is announced the same day that exploit code for that vulnerability is available.

CHAPTER 12 Other Chinks in the Armor

One stone kill all the bird.

- Unknown Google Engineer

This chapter starts with a pretty funny quote. Once you understand it, it's not so funny. The Google engineer used the phrase to imply that you can't have a monopoly on ingenuity; someone outside of Google could topple them. For our purposes, it means simply that the right attack directed at the right vulnerability could end your business. Most cyber criminals want to set up a symbiotic relationship, bleeding you of money, but not so much that you disappear. There are others, however, that may steal from you with the directed goal of removing you from the marketplace. It's these cyber criminals that you have to fear when you look at miniscule holes and potential exploits.

Unfortunately, there are many chinks in the armor. Quite frankly, they are too numerous to discuss in any detail. This chapter will be extremely brief and will touch on some of the issues you should be aware of. Remember, cyber criminals want to make money. If your system contains a way to make money, whether through stock manipulation or outright theft, the cyber criminal will try it.

ACH Transfers

ACH, also known as the automated clearing house system, is a private electronic network that links banks with one another. Originally the ACH system was designed to facilitate bank to bank transfers, and as such it was originally a closed system. While closed, it was virtually a fraud free environment. Today the ACH network is used to move large numbers of transactions, including consumer to consumer, consumer to business and business to business transactions. The security of a closed network is slightly different from an open public network, and as such, ACH is starting to show some ugly flaws. Unfortunately, most banks and financial services companies have no tools in place to detect fraudulent transactions.

Cyber criminals have realized that what they used to do with checks, they can do with ACH. One recent scam involved a cyber criminal generating random account numbers. For each account he would attempt to deposit one cent. When a deposit cleared, the cyber criminal knew he had a live account, and proceeded to withdraw funds from it. The cyber criminal further protected himself against being caught by running the scam at the beginning of the month, presumably to give him plenty of time before the customer's end of month statement.

Unfortunately for you, the financial services community, ACH poses a huge risk. Current law gives a customer 60 days to dispute an ACH debit. A business receives a mere 48 hours to dispute the transaction. At the end of the day, the financial services company will be left holding the bag.

Tools & Tips: Protecting accounts from ACH fraud is pretty straightforward. Your systems should be set up to allow debit blocks on accounts where customers don't require debits. This step minimizes the number of accounts that can be attacked. On accounts that have debit enabled, a variety of bank filtering products can help you. You can white list authorized debitors, or simply impose debit size limits. Companies should watch debits in order to catch unauthorized activity. ACH transactions simply move money to another bank account. They are relatively easy to fix, if caught in time.

Wire Transfers

Wire transfers are very similar to ACH. They are very popular with cyber criminals because once the funds have been wired they are extremely difficult to get back. Many wire transfer companies also offer near-immediate access to the funds for a higher transaction fee. Which the cyber criminals are more than happy to pay, since they are paying with ill-gotten gains. The main problem is that wire transfer companies have no liability; illegitimate transactions are no different to them than legitimate ones. If your firm offers outbound wire transfers, any money wired out of a compromised account on your system is as good as gone. This practice is unlikely to change as wire transfer companies make a fee regardless of the legitimacy of the transaction.

Unfortunately for your firm, the typical cyber criminal has mastered both wire transfers and ACHs. A typical ACH transfer will be to a different account within the same bank the user uses. The account will likely be titled the same. Wires are often labeled with the customer's name, as there are ways to cash it out regardless of the name on the transfer.

Tools & Tips: As you would with ACH transfers, do not enable wire transfers for an account unless explicitly instructed to do so by the customer. For additional protection, allow white lists of valid destinations for those wires. Due to the increased cost of wire transfers, most clients have a short list of destinations.

Client Identification

If your firm is in the financial services industry, it likely requires that an applicant confirm his or her identity through third-party documentation. Your firm will likely request a copy of the applicant's driver's license, passport or utility bill. Unfortunately for you, there are services on the Internet that allow you to quickly create counterfeits of any of these documents. Web sites such as Scanlabs.name and others can create scans of the following documents - many for under $30 a piece:

- Credit Cards (Visa, Mastercard, Maesto/ Cirus, Amex, Discover)

- Passports (US, Europe, Russia and others)
- Driver Licenses (US, Europe, Russia, and others)
- Statements (credit cards and bank accounts)
- Bills (phone, electric and others)
- Certificates (birth, marriage, divorce, death)
- Diplomas (colleges, etc)
- Checks

At a minimum, employ additional checks to verify that the names listed on the applicant's documents match up with other third party sources.

Web Services

Web services are all the rage. They are simply pieces of software that allow two machines to talk to each other. Typically, these services are web APIs accessible over the Internet. In the financial services world, web services provide the same functionality that your web site provides to your clients. These systems exist so that third parties and automated systems may interface with your site.

The main problem is that, unlike fat clients that can run JavaScript, Flash, and other extensions that may help you fight fraud by fingerprinting the computer, web services don't have those extensions. Think of web services as a command line access to your web site. You are left with two data points: the computer's IP address and the transaction. No other passed data is trustworthy. If your API asks the name of the software interfacing with it, a cyber criminal could easily spoof the answer. Your best method for protecting your web service is to make it an opt-in system. A client must request access to the web service in order for it to be active on the client's account. For those users that **are** active, implement behavior systems to detect anomalous transactions. Short of those two solutions, there isn't much to work with.

Micro-payment Theft

Micro payment theft is a relatively new trick in the cyber criminal's bag. The threat, unfortunately, is real. When you setup a brokerage account, you have the option to link it via ACH to your bank account. The brokerage will confirm that this is your account by sending you several small payments under a dollar. You then confirm the amounts on the website. Once this process is done, the ACH link is set up. You can effortlessly transfer money between the two accounts. If you have been thinking out of the box, then you should realize the flaw in this system. If a cyber criminal could register thousands of brokerage accounts and create ACH links to multiple bank accounts, he could quickly amass a substantial amount of money with all those sub-dollar transactions. Once the micro-payments were sent to the bank, the cyber criminal could just transfer the money to a cash card and walk away with it. Imagine how much money could be made by simply registering a few thousand accounts. The threat, unfortunately, is real and has claimed a number of large companies.[71]

IVR

Interactive Voice Response systems are always a weak point for an organization. Typically, an IVR system exposes the same functionality available on the web site through a series of automated menus. It's rare that they are as well-protected. For example, if you use secure tokens on your web site, do you require that your client enter his token when he accesses the IVR? If the cyber criminal is able to assemble the right information, he could request a PIN reset for the IVR system. Once this is done, you may have little to no defense. Sites like Spoof-Card.com, TeleSpoof.com, Itellas.com and others, allow cyber criminals to buy cheap phone cards and spoof their phone numbers to match your client. These cards make calls essentially impossible to trace. When you get past the spoof company, the originating number is often a Skype phone or disposable cell phone.

---

71. Poulsen, Kevin. "Man Allegedly Bilks E-trade, Schwab of $50,000 by Collecting Lots of Free 'Micro-Deposits'." Wired, May 27, 2008. http://blog.wired.com/27bstroke6/2008/05/man-allegedly-b.html.

Your best method to combat fraud through IVR is to watch for password resets followed by suspicious account activity. You should always alert your client via email when a PIN reset occurs. You could also put some information on your web site letting the user know when activity in his account has occurred via the IVR system.

Social Engineering Staff

Social engineering is so prevalent that your own client support representatives may become your biggest weakness. With cyber criminals doing more and more research, you should assume that they have the user's full credit report and as much personal information as can be acquired. Additionally, when cyber criminals call, a spoof card will ensure that your call center sees the proper phone number on your Caller ID system. Training can increase the ability of your call center representatives to identify manipulation. Educate your call center as to the tactics of social engineers and the technology they have at their disposal. Hold quarterly refreshers in some form. It's always best if you can use actual calls that you have received by cyber criminals. Cyber criminals do not make one attempt to get in, giving up if they are stopped. They repeatedly call back with different accounts hoping to get a rep that lets them in. Because of their persistent nature, it's often possible for your representatives to recognize the voice of the attacker.

Front Running

A broker who executes his own trades before executing those of his customers is committing the illegal practice known as "Front Running". After the customer's orders are executed, the broker can close out his position for a guaranteed profit. Profits can be made on both sides; on the buy side by buying the security before the client, or on the sell side by shorting the security before selling the clients. For purposes of this book, it would be possible for a piece of malware to delay large orders and notify the cyber criminal. The cyber criminal could then front run your clients order and make a guaranteed profit. This type of attack would be extremely hard to detect. You likely would only be able to detect it if you had your client on the phone and were watching the order book when they placed the order. It's possible that a tool such as Mantas may be able to detect the front running, but only if the cyber criminal's account and the clients account were both located at your firm.

Accomplices/Moles

No firm likes to think that it's possible that an accomplice or mole has infiltrated their ranks. However, when there are large sums of money to be made anything is possible. The simplest way to use a mole would be to front run positions, while this is relatively easy to catch if the beneficiary is a

single account, one front run execution per individual would be difficult to catch.

Collusion

Collusion is defined as a secretive agreement
between two or more parties in order deceive, mis-
lead or defraud others. It's likely your firm has
been the victim of collusion many times but you
were either unaware of it or unable to track it
down. The common scenario is that a customer
will hand his credentials to another party and have
them initiate a risky position in a security. The customer will then monitor the price of this security
via some other quote service, and be careful not to
login to their account since logging in would
require they immediately report the "unauthorized" login and purchase of the security. If the
risky position pays off, they simply log in and liquidate the position. If the position takes a loss,
which is more likely the case, the customer logs in
and then reports the unauthorized activity. With
most brokers offering security guarantees they will
simply check the login records, seeing a strange IP,
and then correct the clients account by putting the
money back that existed before the unauthorized
security purchase. Obviously this can only be
done once, but that's once per client per firm.

Ticker Manipulation

Ticker manipulation, or quote feed manipulation, hasn't been seen, however, it may be a future avenue of attack. If the cyber criminal can get a piece of malware onto the systems of either high value clients, such as advisors, or onto users that use automated systems then he should be able to manipulate the quote feed they are seeing. In the case of clients, they may be able to get the user to liquidate or purchase large blocks of securities which will impact the price. While the control they wield isn't as precise as a pump-and-dump, it could be just as effective. In the event the user has an automated system, the control is exacting. The largest issue with this attack is that proving it occurred or didn't occur is difficult for either side.

Simulation of Attack

Simulated attacks are interesting since they are just that, simulations. Simulations do not provide revenue to the cyber criminal. However, a believable simulation, which could involve using hundreds of accounts buying dozens of securities in a short period of time, could distract your fraud team enough that the real attack designed to be profitable gets lost in the noise. While the simulation would use quite a few accounts, these days account credentials are abundant.

Targeted Attacks

Cyber criminals are already targeting users by scraping the balance positions of pages. The more money in the account the more likely the account will be used. However, an interesting take would be to specifically target very high net worth individuals, such as CEOs and political figures. These accounts would literally be the cream of the crop, firms should partition these accounts out and apply extra precautions around them since not only could they lead to large losses, but the fallout could lead to bad press.

Open Network Access

I'm going to lump a broad category of things under this section. By open network access, I mean access to your internal network. It is a great deal easier for a cyber criminal to steal huge sums of money once he has a connection inside your network. You must do everything you can to make sure that such a connection never occurs.

Wireless networking is one of the greatest enabling technologies around. When you implement it, make absolutely sure that you use every available technology to secure it. If you aren't using everything from MAC filtering on up, then you need to review your wireless implementation. Better yet, hire an outside pen test company to attempt to breach your wireless network.

Multifunction Printers

Multifunction printers are both a cost-saver and a curse. MFPs these days contain everything from web servers, to email accounts, to hard drives. If an attacker can breach an MFP, it's likely that he could go undetected for a long period of time. After all, who even patches MFPs?

Kiosks

Kiosks put in place by your company are always a tough one; if they aren't on a completely isolated network, with isolated gear, and physically locked down, then they are a threat. Configuration mistakes can expose your internal network. Personnel in the area of the kiosks can prevent their misuse by a cyber criminal by simply confronting the user. Most cyber criminals like to keep a low profile and will simply walk away without achieving their goal.

Terms

Caller ID – Caller Identification, or more properly calling number identification. It is sometimes called calling line identification when provided by a private branch exchange (PBX) system. It is a service provided by your phone carrier that transmits the caller's phone number to the destination telecommunications equipment during the ring.

Flash – Adobe Flash, a technology that allows for multimedia on a website.

IVR – Interactive Voice Response. IVR is a technology that allows a computer program to detect voice and the touch tones of a phone during a phone call. Typically the interface is a series of menus that the user can navigate to get to the feature or person they want.

JavaScript – A scripting language developed by Netscape, it allows the addition of interactive and dynamic content to a webpage.

Kiosks – A stand-alone, self contained unit that houses a computer screen, keyboard and mouse. Typically a kiosk is used for getting onto the Internet.

PIN – Personal Identification Number. A PIN is typically a short sequence of digits used to verify the user or the holder of a token

Skype – A software program that allows users to make phone calls over the Internet to other Skype users, land lines and cell phones.

CHAPTER 13 Future Attack

When it comes to the future, there are three kinds of people: those who let it happen, those who make it happen, and those who wonder what happened.

- John M. Richardson, Jr.

Predicting trends in the computer industry is one of the most difficult undertakings any writer can pursue. One can liken this momentous task to that of fortune telling. Fortune tellers, however, may have more information at their fingertips. Despite that fact, this author will attempt not only to give you an idea of where attacks are headed, but also to provide a rough timeline of when these attacks will be deployed. This timeline attempts to predict when a specific attack or technology will first appear. From the cyber criminal side, these tools and technologies will eventually migrate into point and click tool kits that anyone willing to pay can use. This timeline is based on best guesses and any disruptive technology on either side could radically shift these predictions.

Year: 2008

Two thousand and eight will be the start of some interesting attacks. The first thing you will notice, a trend that started late 2007, is attacks directed against high value assets. Instead of using large numbers of accounts with very little money, a sure sign of a pump-and-dump, attackers will use a few accounts with sufficient funds to execute an attack. Attackers can identify high-value accounts by scraping the balance screen or taking a snap shot of it when the malware grabs the user's credentials to a site. This trend should continue until tools are put in place to thwart this behavior. Assuming the behavior can be thwarted, it's likely to return in later years with fully automated attacks.

This year we will see more financial services companies move towards enhanced authentication systems such as those provided by RSA's Adaptive Authentication and VeriSign's Identity Protection. These systems work by fingerprinting your client's computer, using various data points such as IP address, screen resolution, color depth, etc. If the fingerprint of the current computer doesn't match what's on record for your account, the site asks additional knowledge-based challenge questions. Access is granted once these challenge questions are correctly answered. Cyber criminals shouldn't have too many issues with these types of systems. Unfortunately, if a user's personal computer is compromised and giving away user credentials, then it's likely that the malware will also grab the answers to the secret questions. If you believe the numbers from Chapter 2, then it's likely that 16%-25% of your users will lose their questions and answers when they initially sign up. Additionally, the more frequently the user is challenged the more quickly their secret questions will be compromised. With that in mind it's safe to assume that these tool sets are likely to reduce losses by 40%-60%. While that sounds like a lot, if the attacks against you double, then you are only delaying the upward trend for a year, before it starts to increase again. What's worse is that from 2005-2007 your losses have likely more than doubled each year.

Assuming the financial services companies have successfully deployed enhanced authentication systems, it's likely that cyber criminals will respond with more sophisticated attacks. The PINCH trojan is already attempting to collect not only RSA/VIP type tokens but also the victim's system information. The attacker will be able to initially locate a proxy close to the victim, and then launch an attack from that computer while closely simulating the victim's computer. The goal of this attack would be to lower the risk score that these systems create and get below the threshold for a challenge. The likely response by companies would be to tweak that threshold, leading to a far greater number of challenges, leading to greater customer dissatisfaction, and a greater likelihood of a user's complete set of secret questions being stolen. These "enhanced" systems only work so long as they are infrequently used.

The middle of 2008 will see an increase in the number of compromised Apple computers. This increase will be due to the increased market share of Apple, the lack of comparable security products to those available for Microsoft Windows systems, and the attitude of Apple users that their systems are "secure out of the box". Additionally, Apple users are generally elite and thus juicy targets that can be ignored by the cyber criminals for only so long.

Bots should continue to serve as launching pads for attacks, however, as systems develop to share data between financial services companies, it will become more likely a bot will be "burned" after its first use. This change will result in more sophisticated bots that rotate their signatures and IP addresses. Command and control back ends will allow cyber criminals to locate bots as close to the victim as possible through the use of basic geo-location technology. At the start of 2008 the cyber criminal could launch his attack from within the same state as the victim, moving to the same city and possibly even the same ISP. The bot masters' move to P2P technologies will pay off, and not even they will know where all their bots are.

The end of 2008 should see an up tick in malware crafted for specific targets in the U.S. financial services industry. The malware itself will appear in smaller distributions, with higher rates of mutation. This new paradigm will allow larger amounts of malware to stay hidden on user's personal computers for longer amounts of time. In the event of detection, only a single variant will be detected. Any virus pattern designed to remove it will only disrupt a small percent of the cyber criminals' targets.

For cyber criminals, money movement towards the end of 2008 will become more difficult, as financial service companies will begin to share more and more information. Cyber criminals will likely abandon pure money transfers out of brokerage accounts using ACH/Wires. Instead, they will examining more financial instruments, such as options and larger listed stocks, coupled with smaller transaction sizes. As a result, dumpers' accounts will become increasingly difficult to identify.

The move towards attacks launched from the users' personal computer will be likely come to fruition in late 2008. No longer will a bot be needed. The cyber criminal will simply check his command and control console, see which victims' computers are on the Internet, and launch the attack from one or more machines. This tactic will completely defeat systems looking at fingerprints and the like. PRG has already morphed with this capability; it's just a matter of time before it hits the online brokers.

Year: 2009

This author will go out on a limb at this point and make a prediction; it's likely in 2009 that a large broker will disclose a total loss for the year from cyber fraud of more than $50 million dollars. This news will quickly get the attention of regulators. What will be revealed is a large disparity in what brokers are doing to secure their systems from these types of attacks. Cyber criminals should start embracing cloud computing at an accelerated pace. Tool kits should start showing up early in the year making phishing take down a nightmare. Additional stolen credentials will likely be dropped in the cloud making the take down of drop sites nearly impossible.

By 2009 there should be a scramble by financial services companies to layer on additional technology. Small brokers will be able to mandate two factor tokens, which will slow customers. Due to their small size, however, it becomes possible to require the token with each order. Many companies will incorrectly implement the technology. The technology will only provide some benefit if the company allows one use of a given token and requires input of the token with each transaction. An attacker could wait for the entry of the transaction and of the token and then manipulate the entry after the user submits it but before it is sent to the web server through a variety of methods.

Larger brokers will likely turn their efforts towards more behind-the-scenes technology and invest in transactional behavior detection systems. These systems build patterns around the user's trading habits and money movement habits. In addition, challenge questions will be supplemented with out of band technologies. Risky behavior will result in an automated call to the user using a previously specified number; the user will need to enter the pin displayed on the screen for the transaction to continue.

By the end of 2009, we may see the first "protest" attack, where protesters are able to do significant financial damage to a company's stock. The attack may also last several days, causing heavy volume and large price fluctuations in the target company. At the end of the day, brokers will be left holding the bag. The target company should recover within several weeks. Swings in the price of the target stock may be greatly exaggerated by fears of a follow-up attack.

Year: 2010 and Beyond

Assuming that everything predicted thus far has happened, cyber criminals have stepped up their game. At the same time, hardware manufactures have started putting security technology into processors and motherboards. A new version of Windows will be out, and a newer, more secure, array of browsers is shipping.

It's likely the cyber criminals will have moved to advance data gathering, gathering not only the user's credentials and challenge questions, but also their transaction history. This information will allow the cyber criminal to perform pump-and-dump attacks with securities that the user is likely to trade. If the cyber criminal is successful at data gathering, he could determine which stocks to pump, and how many shares to buy in each account without alerting transactional behavioral systems. The cyber criminal's trades merge seamlessly into the noise of daily trading. Such an approach would require more accounts, but it would allow the cyber criminal to use each account to its maximum value, rather than just concentrating on high value accounts as he did in late 2007 and into 2008.

Additionally, malware will advance to the point of being able to automatically steal money from the user while making the balances in the accounts appear to be unchanged. This deception will be accomplished initially by malware that uses a local proxy to rewrite the inbound HTML, but it will eventually morph into complex code injection that can provide the same functionality.

Since I went out on a limb for 2009, I may as well go out on further limbs. By the end of 2010, conventional pattern matching anti-virus systems will be completely dead. Their effectiveness will have fallen below 50%. While the anti-virus industry will not have been technically defeated, their business models will have been essentially killed. By this date, anti-virus vendors will have likely moved to behavior systems in their products.

CHAPTER 14 Countermeasures

To fight and conquer in all your battles is not supreme excellence; supreme excellence consists in breaking the enemy's resistance without fighting.

- Sun Tzu

The question by now has to be, "What can I do to stop everything that is happening?" To some degree, the answer is, "Not much." Technology has not kept pace with the cyber criminals. We are, unfortunately, at a distinct disadvantage.

As a company, you have two major problems. First you essentially have only defensive capabilities, while our enemy has both offensive and defensive capabilities at his disposal. Second, according to game theory, in order to defeat an unmitigated attack you will have to change your defensive posture faster than the cyber criminal can analyze your defenses, formulate an attack and execute. Given the protean nature of the enemy, developing such a rapidly evolving defense is extremely difficult.

Additionally, many vendors claim that they understand the fraud issue and have fixed the problem. In reality, few vendors grasp the issue, and even fewer have a clear vision for fixing the problem. In this chapter, we are going to look at a range of technologies being promoted as the fix - and why they aren't. We will then examine some promising technologies to see if they can save the Internet.

Authentication

Authentication is an interesting issue. Many guidelines and products have come out in recent years focused on "fixing" the authentication problem. What no one tells you is that there is not an authentication issue per se. After all, it is in the vendor's best interest to leave this little bit of information out of his presentation. Your client base is not having their user ids and passwords brute forced. Criminals are simply intercepting them before they even reach your web site. They may be sniffing the keyboard, stealing the posted data, or using over a dozen other methods. Worse yet, they may be using multiple techniques to guarantee they get the information they want. According to the Anti Phishing Working Group, there are between 200 and 300 unique key logger variants released each month. The SANS Institute, a security professional training group, paints an even grimmer picture by estimating that as many as 9.9 million US personal computers are infected with key logging software. These infected computers contain a low-ball estimate of $24 billion dollars in bank account assets.

If you are not convinced about the password strength of the common user, a recent attack on MySpace accounts demonstrated the surprising integrity of users' passwords. On average, a selected password was eight characters in length. Eighty-one percent of the passwords were alphanumeric, though 28% of those were lowercase plus a single final digit. Sixty-six percent of the time, the digit was the number one. On the plus side, fewer than 4% of the passwords were in the dictionary.[72]

These numbers are certainly better than corporate America, especially when you look at a recent study of employee passwords. Their passwords averaged 7.8 characters in length, with 78% alphanumeric.[73] MySpace is inhabited by a younger crowd, certainly younger than the corporate America crowd. Clearly, younger people understand what a password does, and how to craft a relatively strong one at that.

Layering additional authentication will not fix the problem, but it may slow some cyber criminals for a short time. Fraud will temporarily drop, however it's questionable if your ROI will ever be reasonable, not to mention that this type of technology typically annoys your clients to no end. You also have to be cognizant that most additional authentication systems require distribution, management, and additional call center support. Be sure to include these factors and other spends in your ROI calculation. These costs always add up to a number greater than the purchase price of the product.

This author would like to offer up a hypothesis; given a new authentication scheme, a user will do the least amount of work to pass the authentication scheme. This hypothesis can be demonstrated

72. Schneier, Bruce. "Real World Passwords." Schneier.com. http://www.schneier.com/blog/archives/2006/12/realworld_passw.html.

73. Fredstie, Øyvind, End Users Attitudes and Behaviors towards Password Management: Survey Report, 2006.

with even basic passwords. If the requirement is an alphanumeric password, the user will pick a word followed by one numeric character. For example, you might see "kittens1". Few, if any, users will select something more complex, like "Kv141337R0z".

In the rest of this section we discuss authentication technologies and attempt to highlight issues that can significantly affect your ROI.

IP Geolocation

IP Geolocation involves the mapping of IP addresses to geographic locations. As you can imagine this data is very volatile. Most companies that provide this data continuously update it. For authentication, a geolocation system compares to the location of with the current login attempt with historical login locations. Based on this information, an authentication would be allowed to proceed, or a stronger form of authentication would be required. These systems also work with black and white lists that allow you to always block or allow certain IP addresses. More advanced versions of these systems also calculate a "ground speed" to determine if a user could have physically moved from his previous location to his current login location. This system tends to create a large number of false positives when a user uses third-party consolidators or proxy servers.

Beating IP Geolocation

Beating geolocation is pretty straightforward. Once an attacker installs malware onto the user's computer, he can determine its IP address. The attacker can then rent a bot that is physically near the target's computer, tricking your geolocation system. Newer trojans also allow for the launch of an attack directly from the users PC, bypassing the issue altogether.

Device Authentication

Device Authentication, sometimes called machine authentication, works by looking at several factors on the computer to create a unique device fingerprint. Once the fingerprint is created, the security system places a token on the device in the form of a cookie or flash object. When the user returns, the system validates the token to see if it has been paired to the account logging in. If the token isn't valid or hasn't been paired to that account, the system either assigns an elevated risk score or asks for additional authentication. Device authentication is typically paired with a knowledge-based challenge system, one time password token, one time password list, grid authentication system or out of band authentication system.

Unfortunately, with a large user population, some interesting statistics emerge. In a given month, you will see the following results emerge in your population.

Anecdotal evidence from some large installations has shown some interesting statistics. Typically, the fingerprint cookie is missing on 10% of the sessions that connect to you. Between anti-spyware software, public kiosks, and sandbox applications, the user might have deleted, rejected, and reset any cookies you provide. About 3% of the sessions will come from a brand new user-agent field, which gives information about the operating system and browser running on the PC. New user-agents fields can be caused by browser upgrades or changes. Surprisingly, you will see roughly 11% of your users coming from new IP addresses due to their ISP expiring their prior address. Roughly 2.1% of the sessions will originate from a location the user hasn't visited before due to travel or the use of proxies. When implementing a large user population (>1,000,000 users), assume at least a 6%-8% challenge rate, due to the issues above. If a vendor quotes you a lower number, be suspicious.

Beating Device Authentication

Device authentication has several issues that can render the system useless. The main avenue of attack is to simply piggyback on the user's authentication. PRG and other trojans can simply wait for the user to authenticate to make any transactions.

A simpler attack would be to place a trojan on the user's machine and collect the user's credentials. As long as the user's machine is powered on and connected to the Internet, the attacker could strike at his convenience. Since the user would have paired his machine to his account, a challenge would not typically occur. The attacker would be performing typical trades from the user's own machine.

The second avenue of attack is more theoretical, as it has not yet appeared. There are trojans, such as PINCH, that steal not only credentials and system information, but the device cookie used by these device authentication systems. Attackers are likely trying to beat upcoming deployments of device authentication systems. In device authentication systems, the device fingerprint is derived from data points such as screen resolution and color depth. To avoid detection, it may be possible to simulate the exact settings of the victim's computer. While the IP address may not match, the attacker could get close enough (same city, same ISP) to appear as an IP change due to DHCP expiration. At that point, the system looks for the cookie, which may not exist due to the user clearing it out, so the system attempts to recreate it by looking at the matching system information. Since the criminal has created a mirror image of the victim's computer, it's likely the machine will be allowed through. This approach won't generate a perfect match, but it's good enough to stay under the alert threshold. This vulnerability exists because the web server relies on the client running a piece of code and returning the results. In this situation, it's possible to short-circuit the process, passing back whatever data the attacker wishes.[74] A manual version of this attack would look something like the example below:

Collect Intelligence from the Target Site

1. Browse to the target web site.

2. In the site's login form, view source and look for the script that collects device parameters, if no script is found then it likely uses HTTP headers

3. Use script to collect the same parameters and HTTP headers on the victim's machine

4. Collect all cookies and flash files associated with the target site

Launch the Attack

1. Put all cookies and flash files from the victim's machine on the attacking machine

---

74. O'Connor, Brendan. "Greater than One: Defeating "strong" authentication in web applications." http://www.roysac.com/blogimages/dc-15-oconnor.pdf (paper presented at DefCon 2007 Las Vegas, Nevada, Aug 8, 2007).

2. Install a local proxy that allows you to control and edit the requests that your browser sends to the website (such as Paros[75])

3. Change your HTTP headers to match the headers you collected from the victim's machine

4. Browse to the target web site

5. Once the login form presents script for collecting the device parameters, manually provide the data collected from the victim's machine

This attack is sufficient to get under most thresholds. A more sophisticated attacker would also collect IP, ISP and Organizational information, allowing the attacker to match those parameters with a bot. A company's only defense would be to increase the sensitivity of their device authentication thresholds, creating more false positives. In the event this system is paired with some form of additional challenge system, the increase in false positives would create an increase in challenges, annoying customers and accelerating the capture of secret questions on any machine with a keylogger.

---

75. Paros. http://sourceforge.net/projects/paros/.

Knowledge-Based Authentication

Knowledge-based authentication systems are all the rage. Unfortunately, in the time that it has taken for firms to embrace this technology, it has already defeated. This technology attempts to enhance a user's password by asking additional challenge questions in high-risk situations. These questions are typically knowledge-based in the form of "What was the make of your first car". Several hurdles lay in the path of any institution implementing this type of system.

The largest challenge lies in creating a corpus of questions with memorable answers that are not easily researched by the attacker. You should assume that the attacker has a large amount of resources and can easily research the most basic questions. If your site contains any personally identifiable information, you're already in trouble. For example, if your site contains tax forms, they may contain social security numbers or if you display the user's address, the complexity of your task has increased by orders of magnitude. If the attacker can acquire the address or the social security number of his target, he is now capable of searching everything from birth records to marriage records. He can even construct a quick family tree. This information immediately eliminates questions such as "Who is your favorite aunt/ uncle?" etc. The attacker could search property records, answering questions around where the person lived at various times. When used in conjunction with the family tree, the attacker could answer questions like "What is the name of the grammar school you attended?" Questions about loans you have held or property that you have owned quickly dissolve with this information.

Now that you have eliminated easy-to-remember questions, you must examine the question pool. A good question is one known only to the owner of the account, with a large number of possible answers. For example, a bad question would be "What's your favorite color?". It's an easy one for the attacker; statistically 72% of women will answer blue, purple or green and 80% of men will answer blue, green or black. With 3 guesses, an attacker can access most accounts. The issue, however, is much worse. An attacker doesn't need all the answers to all the users he has harvested. He needs a very small amount. If an attacker has compromised 100 accounts, he will need to use just a handful to carry out his nefarious plans.

Another subtle issue is the tracking of used challenge questions. This information is important for not only forensic analysis, but also for determining when to force the user to pick a new set of questions. As a user uses each challenge question, the likelihood that it has been compromised increases until the point where all questions are considered compromised. Let us assume for a second that 5% of all computers in the United States are compromised with key logging capable software. If a user uses a challenge question, there is a

5% chance that it has been compromised. After the challenge question has been used ten times on twenty different machines, then based on the following formula:

$$[1 - (1 - 0.05 \times Q_{ask} / Q_{total})^n]$$

Where:

n = the number of unique machines the user has been challenged on

Q_{ask} = the number of questions that the user can pick from to answer for a challenge (if only one question is displayed and cannot be advanced then the value is 1, if the user can advance through all questions then the answer is Qtotal)

Q_{total} = the number of challenge questions the user answered at enrollement

There is approximately a 64% chance that the challenge has been compromised after twenty logins. At this point, the question should be reset. The more challenge questions you have chosen for a user to complete, the longer the life of the question set. Two questions are likely good for forty challenges, and four questions are likely good for eighty-two challenges, assuming the conservative 5% compromise number.

Failure to prevent advancement to a new question can severely impact the life of a set of challenge questions. For example if a user has four challenge questions in his pool, but two are displayed to the user, the effectiveness is the same as that of an overall pool of two questions. If you allow a user to advance through all four questions without successfully answering them, then the effectiveness drops to that of a single question. If you allow the attacker to advance, the attacker has a better chance of reaching a compromised question.

If your organization is looking at utilizing a 3rd party knowledge based archive, you should be aware that you will likely be in worse shape than if you select your own questions. First, this knowledge is typically researchable since it is usually based on public information; however the root issue is that answers can be researched with zero prior knowledge. These systems work by passing your system a question with multiple choices for the answer. By simply getting challenged multiple times with the same question you can figure out the correct answer since for a given question there is one correct answer followed by several random incorrect choices. If I were to ask you, "How much is your mortgage payment on your house?" your first set of choices might be "A) $1591 B) $2374 C) $1821". In another iteration you might see "A) $2374 B) $2184 C) $1937". Comparing the two sets, it becomes obvious that the correct answer to the question is $2374.

Another easy way to attack a multiple choice system is to simply grab a screen shot of the question and answers along with either a keystroke or the position of the mouse when the answer is selected. Of course that solution actually requires a small amount of work.

Even worse, a system like this does a great disservice to your customer. A knowledge based archives discloses information about your customer that you don't store, thereby allowing a more complete theft of a person's identity.

Beating Knowledge Based Authentication

Assuming a company can come up with a set of questions that can't be researched; the avenue of attack is straightforward. The attacker simply needs to erase the cookies and flash objects associated with your site from the victim's computer. The attacker then alters the victim's user agents. Instead of the user having Microsoft Internet Explorer, it now appears that he has Firefox. These changes will trigger a challenge to the user. When the user is challenged, the cyber criminal simply steals the question and answer. In a few logins, the attacker will have successfully stolen all the user's secret questions and answers. The problem then becomes one of authenticating your users when they call in. The attacker likely already knows or can research the user information you may have. Now that he has private information about your client, your job is nearly impossible. The more connected we are, the fewer secrets we have.

One-Time Password Tokens

One-Time password token systems, or OTP for short, are systems that use small hardware tokens known as key fobs as an extra piece of authentication validation. Software versions of this technology are becoming more popular, though they suffer from additional issues if the software is running on the same system as the user's browser. Software fobs running on devices such as cell phones, Blackberries and PDAs are just as secure as the standalone hardware key fobs, since it's unlikely a cyber criminal would successfully attack any of these systems.

Tokens come in two main flavors, time-synchronized and challenge-based.

The basic concept behind time-synchronized tokens is that a user is given a key fob that displays a unique sequence of digits. This number changes at a fixed interval, typically every 30 or 60 seconds, and is used in conjunction with a static user id. The issuer of the token is capable of predicting the displayed code for any user at any given time due to the fact that the token and the server are synchronized. The idea is that even if your user id and password are stolen, the cyber criminal would have to access your account within the 30 or 60 second time interval to access your account. This time window was believed to be far too short for the cyber criminal, and therefore impossible to break. In reality, this system is impossible to brute force, which, as we will see, is not the same thing.

Challenge/response tokens work slightly differently, in that they require some form of input into them along with an internal counter, which is used to generate the unique token. The main problem with this system is that passwords are not time-synchronized and remain valid for long periods of time. These passwords are more susceptible to phishing than time-synchronized passwords.

Both of these methods sound great, and they likely take low-level cyber criminals out of the game until a tool kit to defeat them arrives. Ultimately, these tokens do little, since no financial institutions have properly implemented them. Worse, some financial services companies in the banking sector implemented OTP tokens to comply with the Federal Financial Institutions Examination Council (FFIEC) recommendations for two-factor authentication.

One time password systems' viability came into question after a phishing attack was launched against Citibank, late in 2006. Security professionals have known for a while that OTP systems were susceptible to man-in-the-middle attacks. There was little surprise to security professionals when the news broke.

A major issue with these token based systems is that you need to manage physical tokens and securely deploy them to your users. Problems do crop up with these tokens, such as tokens falling out of sync or the token simply wearing out. You must also plan a contingency for a user that forgets or misplaces his token and still needs to transact business with you. If third parties connect to you on behalf of the client, you have another can of worms. In the financial services industry, consolidator services such as Yodlee[76] will become a thorn in your side. If your company allows transactions to occur through a web service or other published API, you cannot guarantee that there is a user on the other end. As soon as you deploy a work-around, cyber criminals will attempt to exploit the hole you opened to solve these issues. These problems pile up quickly with token use. As complexity grows, your returns diminish.

Beating One-Time Passwords

To defeat one-time passwords, there are two attack vectors you can use. The first, long known, is to use a man-in-the-middle attack. A cyber criminal will use a phishing attack to get the client's data. Once the victim clicks on the bogus link, he is redirected to a convincing fake web site. At this point, the cyber criminal has two choices. First, the cyber criminal can accept the credentials and the

76. Yodlee. http://www.yodlee.com.

token. In the case of a time-synchronized token, this choice would trigger an alert back to the cyber criminal so the token can be used immediately. Alternatively, the cyber criminal can act as a passive intermediary, connecting to the real web site on the users behalf. This approach allows the cyber criminal to observe all of the user's transactions, inject new commands, and control data displayed to the user. An example appears in the figure below (Figure 14-1).

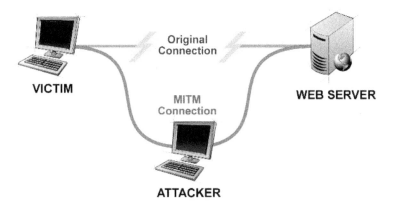

Figure 14-1 Man-in-the-Middle

An attacker could use an in-browser attack to accomplish the same thing. Instead of redirecting the user to a proxy or other system, he could simply intercept communications before they are encrypted by the browser. Ultimately, a man-in-the-browser attack is more dangerous, as you may not be able to validate its existence until you get a copy of the malware.

The second main attack vector takes more work, but allows some interesting variations. If the cyber criminal has infected the user's computer, he can infiltrate an authenticated session and start injecting whatever he needs. For example, a trojan can sit on the user's machine watching for the moment he goes to https:\ \www.mybank.com. Once the user logs in, the trojan can perform whatever actions the cyber criminal wants. This ability already exists in the latest version of PRG. If you morph this attack and look forward, this capability is moving toward a command and control system. For example, the trojan could go to google.com and query for some unique string. If the trojan finds the string, it can go to the website listed on the results page. The page could contain a simple command for the trojan. The command might be something as straightforward as "BUY 100 IBM 1/ 10/2009 9:30". The trojan would read and remember the command. If the user was logged in and authenticated at 9:30 AM on January 10, 2009, the trojan would activate and place an order for 100 shares of IBM. Once the command was given, the trojan would lie in wait, verifying its orders right before executing the purchase. Although many users wouldn't be logged in, a significant portion might, especially at the market open. If the cyber criminal was more savvy, he could alter the times for each agent that checked in, further concealing a pump-and-dump scam. Without one-time passwords on each and every transaction, this attack is extremely dangerous. While it has not yet appeared in the wild, companies should be braced for it, as it takes little knowledge or effort to deploy.

Requiring an OTP on each transaction appears on the surface to be a solution, however it presents major issues. In the case of a time-synchronized token, if the time between the login and transaction, or from one transaction to another isn't sufficient, then the token is still using the same code. An attacker could still attack immediately after login. The solution would then be a challenge/response token. If the user has the ability to advance the token, then each generated token can be discarded after use, requiring a new token with each transaction. If properly implemented, with authentication at the transaction level, the cyber criminal would have to use some sort of man-in-the-browser or phishing type attack to be successful. It's very unlikely any company would implement this strategy, since it places an incredible burden on the user. Keep in mind that this strategy is not foolproof. While it may stop pump-and-dump activity, an attacker could substitute the user's fund transfer with his own during submission of the user's request.

One-Time Password Lists

One time password lists are a simplified version of one time password tokens. These were developed in order to reduce cost. A brokerage house sends a list of randomly generated passwords to a user on a card with some form of index. Some of the more 'advanced' cards use scratch-offs to protect the passwords. When the site requires stronger authentication, say for the movement of a large amount of money, the user is prompted to enter the password that appears on a specific line of the card (Figure 14-2). To reduce the chance of these passwords being phished, or taken via man-in-the-middle, the OTP a password on a given line is only used once

	Code Sheet	
Fund Transfer Confirmation	Number	One-Time Password
	00001	kc9jgY
You are attempting to transfer $5,000 USD.	00002	Ru432D
	00003	a53Ew2
Please confirm by entering the following code:	...	
	00019	0R33IC
0003: _____	00020	J301jd
Remember that you will not be asked for this Code again. It is recommended that you physically strike it out from your code sheet.		

Figure 14-2 Request to Enter a Password from a One-Time Password List

Due to the fact that the passwords are only used once and there is limited space on a card, it is not possible to use these pre-generated cards for authentication. They are suited to situations where you want extra authentication on a subset of transactions.

Grid/Bingo CardAuthentication Systems

Grid authentication, sometimes referred to as bingo card authentication, is a simpler and more cost effective method of deploying two-factor authentication without the need for deploying physical tokens. Users are sent a security grid card, typically the size of a credit card. The grid contains a random set of numbers and letters in marked columns and rows (Figure 14-3). When a user enters the site, he is asked for his user ID and password. At this point the user asked for several of the alphanumeric characters on his security grid card.

	A	B	C	D	E	F	G	H	I	J
1	B	2	R	0	Y	1	e	6	V	3
2	7	j	9	F	3	q	4	N	9	K
3	L	5	Z	6	A	5	U	0	G	8
4	4	s	1	M	8	D	2	P	1	W
5	c	3	I	8	t	9	X	7	h	1

Serial # 2938583

Figure 14-3 Request to Enter a Password from a Grid Authentication System

While these systems offer additional security, they are weaker than tokens because there are fewer possible combinations. A typical physical token generates a six-digit number, allowing for 1,000,000 possible values, while a grid system must recycle rows and columns. An attacker could eventually reconstruct the card. As the diagram above shows, if an organization prompts for 3 grid locations, it's possible to 'learn' a card in as few as seventeen prompts. In reality the grid locations would be picked at random, requiring more samples, though not as many as you may think. You can calculate the likelihood of an attacker passing a grid card authentication system after key logging the grid entry N times (See following formula).

$$[1 - (1 - G_{count} / T_g)^N]$$

Where:

G_{count} = Grid locations requested at each authentication event

T_g = Size of Grid

N = The number of times the card has been used

Grid systems also allow for simple site-to-user authentication displaying the unique serial number on the user's security grid. Like all site-to-user authentication, however this number can be captured. It is also susceptible to man-in-the-middle attacks.

Out of Band Authentication

Out of band authentication is a very large category. It encompasses any technology where the user id and password are sent on two separate networks. The attacker would have to compromise both networks to login. The primary network would be the web site, and the out of band channel could be anything from a phone call, to SMS, or possibly an email.

These systems tend to remain effective as long as you can get a large portion of your population to use it. User participation is the Achilles' heal of almost any technology.

Beating Out of Band Authentication

These systems are very effective against man-in-the-middle attacks. Unfortunately, these systems are staring to show cracks. Trojans can wait for the user to authenticate before they activate, which would allow an attacker access to an account after the challenge was answered. Out of band systems could be very effective against transaction fraud. Modern cell phones make it possible to send a user an SMS message that displays the pending web transaction, and asking for approval. This system would allow the user to identify any transaction that was rewritten by a malicious trojan. However it's not practical to use this authentication scheme on every transaction, and as soon as you define a threshold, the attacker can simply probe your system to figure out where it is. Eventually, you reach a point where you can no longer lower your threshold since doing so would cause a large number of false positives. The cost in terms of lost business could quickly outweigh any savings gained through fraud prevention. Once the attacker drops into the noise, the system is beaten.

Smart Cards

Smart cards are pocket-sized cards capable of processing information. There are two types of smart cards. The first are memory cards. Memory cards contain a small amount of non-volatile memory and some basic security logic. The second type of card, called a microprocessor card, contains non-volatile memory and a microprocessor. These more advanced cards come with embedded cryptographic hardware that lets you use algorithms such as RSA and 3DES.

The problem with smart cards is that they have a fairly high hardware failure rate compared to other authentication technologies. The chips are printed on flexible plastic cards. The more complex the chip, the larger the size, and the more likely it will break. Card failure could be offset by providing a safe enclosure for the card. Additionally, users will forget or misplace cards, which means they will be calling you to bypass authentication temporarily. All of these factors result in increased call volume and costs. Worse, it could become an exploit for social engineering.

Beating Smart Cards

Smart Cards suffer from the same issues as OTP. When a smart card is used for authentication, the security can never be 100%. If a user's computer is infected with the proper piece of malware, the malware can get between the user and the destination web site. Once in the middle, the malware can modify transactions at will, unnoticed by the user.

Smart cards are far from unbreakable. In their book *Design Principles for Tamper-Resistant Smart Card Processors*, Ross Anderson and Markus Kuhn managed to crack the Dallas DS5002FP Secure Microcontroller, described at the time by one European signals intelligence agency as the most secure processor available for general sale. Worse yet, their attack utilized a pure brute force method running on an off-the-shelf personal computer enhanced with a few hundred dollars of extra hardware.

Client Side Certificates

Client side certificates, also known as personal certificates, were introduced by VeriSign in 1996. A client side certificate allows the holder to encrypt messages and to identify himself to remote web sites. Client side certificates utilize public key cryptography, involving a public key and a private key. The private and public keys are mathematically related, so a user can encrypt a secret using the public key and only I can decrypt it, using my private key. Public key cryptography ultimately depends upon the secrecy of the client's private key.

When you request a personal certificate from one of the many vendors on the Internet, the vendor automatically generates the private key for you and saves it to your computer. When the certificate is generated, you are prompted for a password. This password is used to encrypt the private key when it is saved to your computer. This step reduces the risk that your key will be intercepted if the computer is compromised in the future.

Beating Client Side Certificates

While this system appears to be secure, it is not as secure as one would think. The certificate is secure when stationary on the hard drive. Its security is weakened when a piece of software accesses it. Unfortunately, it is often accessed by one of many bug-filled browsers.

If a cyber criminal can install malware on a user's computer, then it is possible to recover the private key from memory after it has been decrypted. Once your private key has been captured, the attacker can impersonate the user and gain access to the web site that is using the certificate as a method of security. In addition to this major weakness, there have been concerns about the security that Microsoft Internet Explorer uses to encrypt the private key. While the security differs from version to version, some versions of Internet Explorer can be persuaded to export the private key using 40-bit encryption. Forty bits is known to be susceptible to brute force attacks. In addition, users will likely recycle their passwords, or use dictionary words, in which case no level of encryption will protect the private key.

Even if the cyber criminal doesn't have the technical skills to pull off the above attack, his malware could be crafted to execute from the client's machine. If an attack originates from the client's personal computer, their client side certificate will match up and the cyber criminal will have access.

Virtual Keyboards

A virtual keyboard is an application that displays a virtual keyboard or keypad on your screen; instead of typing in your password on your keyboard you "type" it on screen by clicking your mouse on graphic representations of the keys (Figure 14-4).

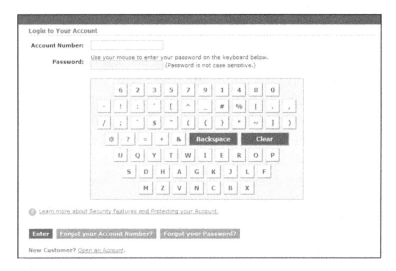

Figure 14-4 Screen Shot of a Virtual Keyboard

Virtual keyboards are enjoying a resurgence in the industry, even though the technology offers nearly no protection against modern malware. Citibank attempted to use this technology, but exploits appeared almost immediately. The technology to defeat virtual keyboards came out in the late nineties in Brazil. You will see many variations of the virtual keyboard claiming to "fix" their inherent issues. Some schemes require you to hover on a key, rather than clicking. Some use keys that randomly change positions. These systems were designed for users with disabilities, not security. As such, they all suffer from the same issues.

Beating Virtual Keyboards

Virtual keyboards have several major flaws. Most virtual keyboards allow the user to enter his password via the graphic display or the hardware keyboard. Unfortunately, as soon as a feature like this is implemented, most users choose the familiar, physical keyboard. As soon as users choose the hardware keyboard, the technology falls prey to keystroke logging attacks. If you disallow hardware keyboard, you may run into issues with users that lack fine motor skills. Of course, the system is troublesome for anyone relies on any form of audio device to navigate.

To maximize the effectiveness of virtual keyboards, the characters must change position with each screen refresh. If the positions are static, malware only needs to gather your screen resolution and mouse position at each click to defeat it. Dynamic key positions are acceptable for a numeric keypad, but a randomly arranged QWERTY keyboard becomes a horrible client experience. Some companies avoid this issue by reverting to a PIN instead of a password, weakening the authentication system further. Some vendors only show a subset of characters. If the characters that aren't part of the password are random, an attacker can eventually determine the characters that do make up the password. Once an attacker has the components of the password, breaking it is trivial.

Even with the random positioning, a piece of malware that can capture a small section of the screen when the mouse is clicked can also defeat the virtual keyboard. Malware that utilizes this technique captures a small amount of the screen with each click for as long as the user remains at a specific URL. The malware then saves this data for later uploading.[77, 78] Files are typically named for the order of the clicks (Figure 14-5).

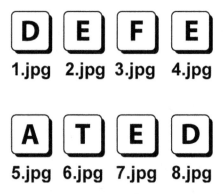

Figure 14-5 Captured Data from a Virtual Keyboard

If the attacker wants to make it even easier for himself, it would be easy to create a compact OCR program within the malware. The OCR program would translate the data prior to sending. Virtual keyboards tend to use very readable text, making this task trivial.

77. Hispasec Sistemas. Cajamurcia-en.swf. http://www.hispasec.com/laboratorio/cajamurcia_en.swf.

78. K.S., Yash. "Defeating Citibank Virtual Keyboard protection using screenshot method." TracingBug.com. http://www.tracingbug.com/index.php/articles/view/23.html.

Additionally, many implementations rely on client side technologies, such as Java or ActiveX. This design decision is dead on arrival. A client side implementation assembles the keys and then sends them back to the web server. An attacker could simply intercept the posted key data. Even if encrypted, the attacker could reverse engineer the code and identify the protection type.

There is no way to fix the security flaws that exist in any implementation of a virtual keyboard. Avoid them unless you would like a large number of unkind security articles written about your company.

Keystroke Biometrics

Keystroke biometrics verify but do not authenticate the identity of a user by using complex statistics to determine if person entering the keystrokes is the user or someone else. These systems measure timings between key presses and key releases, known as "dwell time", along with timings between entries, known as "flight time". A keystroke biometric system may look at which shift key you use when capitalizing certain letters or if a phrase was mistyped and then corrected. The biometric application builds a user template using subsets of these data points. When a user logins in, the keystroke information is compared to the template and a confidence value is returned.

Keystroke biometrics are being used by some companies at the time of login as a second factor to confirm that the user entering the id is in fact the owner of the account. Keystroke biometrics belong to the class of behavior biometrics, not physical biometrics. Behavioral biometrics is not a substitute for physical biometrics since behavioral biometrics relies on statistics. Behavioral biometrics must allow for larger amounts of error, versus physical biometric systems, which have an extremely high confidence level.

These types of solutions tend to accurately confirm the identity of the user, and require no changes to the user's experience. Some solutions are capable of gathering keystrokes without a training session, making the experience even more seamless to the user. The solution is often Flash based, and does not require any additional hardware or software. Even better, the firm does not need to manage or deploy any additional hardware.

Beating Keystroke Biometrics

You may have already guessed that these systems have some weaknesses. Keep several factors in mind when looking at such systems. First, a user will vary his type rate and error rate depending on a number of factors, including time of day, mood, amount of sleep, etc. People are not machines. There are issues that can throw off the speed even further. For example, a user might cut a finger or sprains his wrist. You may run into issues with users that use multiple computers and devices. Different keyboards cause users to perform differently. On the extremes, a user typing on his home PC will have vastly different timings when accessing your site from his PDA while on the phone. Consider both extremes. Your template will have to be forgiving, equaling a loss in accuracy.

If your users share their account information, say with a spouse, then you must maintain multiple patterns for each user id. Each actual user will need to train on the system. Training your users may be an obstacle, however, if your users do not share account information, you can train the system by shadowing the user for a few dozen logins. If your system cannot develop a profile based on shadowing, the training cycle may have a negative impact on user experience. Even worse, you may not know which accounts have shared credentials. While joint accounts and investment clubs are straightforward, you likely have a large number of individual accounts that involve shared user credentials even though they are not flagged as such.

Keystroke biometric systems fail to a variation of a replay attack. A piece of malware could be crafted that records not only characters, but dwell and flight time. Malware could successfully defeat a system by slightly varying these times to avoid

looking like a replay attack. If the malware is sufficiently hidden, the attacker could sample multiple
logins and timings and derive acceptable parameters to defeat any system. Vendors may claim this
exploit cannot occur, but an attacker could simply
craft a virtual keyboard tied to the keyboard
driver. The program would be unable to tell that it
wasn't talking to the real keyboard. The attacker
could then replay the captured keystrokes and timings. Using simple HTML and Javascript
(Figure 14-6) it's trivial to record keystrokes along
with dwell and flight time, one way appears below.
All the attacker would have to do is phish your
users.

```
<script >
var time_start=(new Date()).getTime()/1000;
function grab_n_record(code, type)
{
    var tmp_id = document.getElementById("tmp");
    var curr_time = (new Date()).getTime()/1000;
    tmp_id.innerHTML= tmp_id.innerHTML + "time=" +
    (new Number(curr_time -
    time_start)).toFixed(3)
    + " : ASCII 0x" + code.toString(16) + "(char '"
    +
    String.fromCharCode(code) + "')" +
    " " + "(" + type + ")" + "<br>";
    return;
}
</script>
</head>
<body>
Type text here: <br>
<textarea onkeydown="grab_n_record(event.keyCode,
'Key Down');" onkeyup="grab_n_record(event.keyCode,
'Key Up');"></textarea>
<br>
Keystroke Data is:
<br>
<div id="tmp"></div>
```

Figure 14-6 : JavaScript to Steal Keyboard Biometrics

One major issue with these systems, as with virtual keyboards, is that this system should be implemented on the server side. Any implementation utilizing JavaScript, ActiveX, or any other client side approach, just weakens an already shaky system.

Keyboard biometrics may be useful as an additional factor in helping you determine if your user is on the other side of the session, but do not rely upon it. If malware authors specifically target your company, this technology will become completely ineffective and rapidly so.

Graphical Password Authentication Systems

Graphical passwords are another system that attempts to obfuscate the password by moving from text to graphical representations. There is some evidence that the human brain has an easier time remembering pictures rather than complex strings of random characters. Often the pictures consist of human faces, which the brain apparently has an easier time recalling. The user must identify a sequence of pictures, in this case the faces that he previously selected, in a specific order. The challenge changes with each login attempt, and valid parts of the user password are intermingled with decoys.

While this system allows for greater complexity; rotation of the graphics would likely weaken the password. Only one valid picture would appear on the screen. The rest would be decoys, and subject to rotation. Careful observers could derive the proper pictures. While face recognition is difficult for computers, previously seen static image recognition is not. A computer program does not need to identify an entire picture to break the implementation. By simply sampling a specific set of data points from each selected face, the computer could identify the face and reproduce the proper sequence for login. While a product based on graphics may reduce password resets, it doesn't add to the security of the site. Other vendors have attempted to add in portions of mutual authentication schemes, adding weak security onto an already weak idea.

Beating Graphical Password Authentication Systems

Graphical passwords are really no different from the virtual keyboards discussed previously. These systems fall to the exact techniques as the virtual keyboard. Screen capture around the mouse click is the graphical password system's worst nightmare. Even if you assign random characters to the pictures and ask the user to type the letter under the proper picture, the attack could just capture the screen at key press along with the keystroke.

In addition graphical passwords have at least one flaw that virtual keyboards don't. Instead of a picture of a keyboard, graphical passwords use actual pictures. The only real difference is that if your password is "apple/pear," you may see a picture of an apple, along with other pieces of fruit. You would need to pick the apple displayed on the first screen, the pear on the second, and so on until your password requirements were met. Some systems that utilize this technique have a large flaw in their implementations. They randomize the decoy pictures, allowing you to derive the password without even looking at what the user clicks. In our example above, the next time you log in you may see an apple on the first screen and an entirely different selection of fruit, from that data set you can derive that only the apple was displayed on both screens. Therefore, the apple must be the correct answer.

Draw a Secret (DAS) and Qualitative Draw a Secret (QDAS)

Draw a Secret (DAS) and the variation Qualitative Draw a Secret (QDAS) have been around for quite a while under different names. The concept, however, remains the same.[79] Like many other proposals in the client security world, this solution is experiencing a resurgence. When these systems were conceived, around 1999 and earlier, users and administrators did not understand security, and developed bad habits. Users commonly chose passwords based on dictionary words, without including letters, numbers and case variation. Currently no vendors use this technology on the personal computer side, though there are a few with solutions on PDAs.

The concept is straightforward; a user is presented a grid and is asked to draw a symbol for his

79. Jermyn, Ian, Mayer, Alain, Monrose, Fabian, Reiter, Michael K, and Rubin, Aviel D., "The Design and Analysis of Graphical Passwords," Usenix Security Symposium, city, state, Aug. 1999.

password. The system records the starting point square and all squares that were passed through in sequence. A password may consist of more than one line. So in the diagram below (Figure 14-7), the output for a simple DAS may be {4,1},{3,1}{2,1},{2,2},{2,3},{2,4},{1,4},{1,2},{2,2}. This drawing was my first DAS for this book. Without intending to do so, I immediately encountered issues. For instance, what do you do about the line that goes through 2,4? Technically it's in 2.4, but 2 more pixels and it would have passed through 3,1.

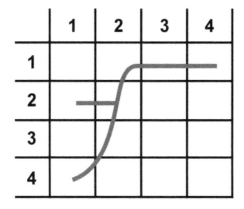

Figure 14-7 DAS Input Grid

QDAS takes the system a step forward by indicating which direction out of the square the line went. While this information should be consistent for the actual user, it's very likely it adds little security. Most users would have two to three lines as a password. The possible combinations are a very short list. Over a few days, an attacker could get the sequence correct without locking out the account. For example, in the drawing above one could conclude that the line starting in grid 2.1 was the second line drawn, since it terminated into the other line. It would be very unlikely that a user would draw that line first, and then attempt to intercept the end point with a second line.

What you see above is the flaw in the system. While papers tout the security of the DAS and QDAS schemes, it seems unachievable in the real world. For example, what do you do about my edge case in grid 2,4? If you ignore it, it's likely my line will be in 1,3 or 2,4 next time. So you either have to reject this password or put in some sort of system that allows for variation. In the first case, you'll annoy users since you are now requiring more precise drawings. In the latter case, you are reducing the password space.

Another test case would be to simply draw an 'X' on the screen. In doing so, you will have the same drift problem encountered by my test figure; it's very likely the user would shift the angle of a line one way or another, causing different output. While I don't disagree with the mathematical calculations of what can be represented, I do think it's unlikely that a user would use all possibilities. For instance, if a user draws a rectangle on a 5x5 grid, it's estimated that there are 2.56×10^6 possible ways that could occur based on direction, number of lines, etc. I, however, believe that most users will go clockwise or counterclockwise using one line. If using 4 lines, the user will draw the top line first, followed by the sides, and then draw the bottom from left to right. It is less likely that a user would choose say to start in the lower right corner, or any other unconventional choice. Predictable behavior greatly reduces the number of passwords.

Beating DAS/QDAS

Beating this system is straightforward. A crafted piece of malware simply waits until user is on the correct screen, and captures all mouse movements and clicks along with the current screen and browser resolution. For an accurate picture of your password, it could take a screen shot when you click the submit button.

Password Managers

Password managers were designed to allow users to store all their passwords in one secure location. A different password for each web site is ideal, but the human mind has difficulty keeping track of large numbers of random characters for any real length of time. The password manager solves that problem by allowing for a global password that can unlock access to all your other passwords. The password manager may be local software that stores your user ids and passwords in a secure vault on the hard drive. The password manager may be a more elaborate system that stores your credentials on a USB device. No matter its form, it's essentially a secure post-it note next to your computer. There are number of these systems on the market. Feature sets and encryption methods vary greatly from product to product. Some systems will even enter your credentials into the web browser for you.

Beating Password Managers

Attackers love password managers. The attacker can target the password manager and just empty the vault. Instead of waiting months for you to login to all of your accounts, he can get those passwords from the vault and steal from you weeks before you would notice. The issue is not with the vault itself. At rest, the passwords are secure. To use them, however, data must move. A password must be entered. While a password is being entered, it is subject to capture either through keystroke grabbing, a memory attack, or some other means. Once that password is compromised, the entire contents of the password vault is lost.

Systems that allow for automatic login don't add any security. For a password manager to log into a site for you, it still must transmit the data the same way you do today. During that transmission, the cyber criminals can capture the credentials. Remember, anything that is automatic for the user is also automatic for the attacker.

There are a few additional popular technologies designed to prevent everything from phishing, bad transaction, and scripting of attacks. These solutions may have some impact on their respective targets typically, but they are still vulnerable to some very easy workarounds.

Phishing protection is obviously important. Phishing is one of the avenues that leads to the loss of your users credentials. If you can lower the likelihood of a user falling for phishing, then you directly reduce your fraud.

Protecting against bad or anomalous transactions may eliminate large number of fraudulent transactions without requiring large changes to your site. For large companies this technology is very attractive.

Protection from scripted attacks is critical. Without protection from scripting, you are vulnerable to denial of service attacks and automated pump-and-dump scams.

Extended Validation Certificates

Extended Validation (EV) Certificates, sometimes known as high assurance certificates, are a relatively new product. EV certificates are a special type of SSL certificate that requires a more extensive background check by the Certificate Authority before being issued. EV certificates thwart phishers by being difficult to acquire and giving visual indicators to the user. A user, when using a modern browser and accessing a site with an EV certificate, will notice that browser displays a green address bar and a special label appears that alternates between the name of the website owner and the Certificate Authority that issued the certificate.

Some inconclusive research shows that the users still can't reliably distinguish a valid site using an EV certificate from a fraudulent site employing various phishing methods. In addition, users that received training about EV certificates were more likely to judge all sites legitimate.

The most likely exploit of an EV certificate is to use a picture-in-picture attack (Figure 14-8). In the picture-in-picture attack, the cyber criminal registers a domain, and creates a web page that not only contains the content but appears to replicate the web browsers' toolbar. This tactic causes confusion for the typical user.

Figure 14-8 Picture-in-Picture Attack

To an untrained user, it appears that he is on a valid EV certified site with multiple browser windows open. The interior window, however, is a fake. With minimal training, users should be able to detect these types of phishing attempts. This exploit suffers from two major giveaways. Both windows are in focus at the same time, and the inner window cannot be maximized.

Site to User Authentication Systems

Site to user authentication systems are designed to protect a user from getting phished by displaying a user selected picture after the user has identified himself, but before he is fully authenticated. As discussed in the phishing chapter, users don't tend to pay attention to this picture. There are several other potential issues, including susceptibility to man-in-the-middle attacks and scalability.

Yahoo demonstrated an interesting spin on this system with their sign-in seal protection. Unlike the standard method of associating the userid with a picture, sign-in seal associates the computer with the picture. This technique has the advantage over the traditional method since when a user connects to the phishing site, there is no obvious way for the phishing site to tell which computer is connecting. By using techniques such as fingerprinting, it would be possible to create a fingerprint of a computer and steal the sign-in seal. Upon connecting to the phish site, a small piece of Java could check the fingerprint of the connecting machine and display the proper seal, defeating the system.

Behavioral Based Systems

Behavioral based systems work by looking at patterns and detecting fraudulent intent. Behavior based systems come in three flavors.

- Access based - These systems look for patterns in user access, such as the time and date the user logs in. The system retrieves log in time and other data points from the HTTP headers.

- Transactional - These systems look for patterns in the security trading. They monitor order sizes, the time of day, the risk of the security, and an endless list of possible data points.

- Behavior - These systems monitor the sequence in which the user performs transaction across and within sessions. For example, is it normal for the user to change his address and then order a new set of checks? This behavior is compared with past user behaviors to locate outliers.

These systems take this data, pass it through some equations, and produce a risk score. The risk score is a probability that the user on the other side is the user of the account. These systems arrive at their conclusions by building complex models of the user's transactions, and comparing those models against models of users with similar behaviors. The system must continuously update the model to be effective. Without constant updates, the system is doing batch training, and your models will always lagging.

Many of the more popular systems rely on multiple technologies, such as Bayesian statistics, neural networks, and deterministic rule sets. We will briefly touch on the three models and what kind of issues you may expect.

Bayesian Statistics

Bayesian statistics is simply a statistical method that incorporates prior knowledge to help calculate the likelihood of something happening. You may have seen vendors advertise spam filters with Bayesian capabilities. The benefit to these systems is that they can continuously update and adapt as new attacks appear. The downside to these systems is that they require a significant amount of fraudulent data and good data to build a model.

If you were modeling authentication events, you would probably want 10 good logins for every bad login. Now you may have deduced the problem. It's possible that cyber criminals have probed your accounts. Because money hasn't gone missing, the login is assumed good. Your training set will contain one group with known fraud and one group with known good logins and unknown fraud. Although this issue is cause for concern, don't discard Bayesian systems. They have the ability to update and "unlearn" the bad data points. You will have a harder time locating a sufficient set of known fraudulent data points upon which to build your statistical model. Some vendors claim that they can get around the issues with a few data points. They are essentially over-training with the data you have, or manipulating the data to train on fraud that never really occurred.

Neural Networks

Neural networks are a simplified mathematical model of biological neural networks, aka your brain. Neural networks excel at finding patterns in data where no apparent patterns exist. They are capable of absorbing a large number of data points and quickly discarding the data that is meaningless. Due to the complexity of the training of these systems, however, it's often difficult to tell what a neural network is focusing on during training.

There is a story from many years ago about the U.S. military attempting to use neural networks to recognize enemy tanks on the battlefield. As the story goes, the researchers trained the system on thousands of pictures that either contained tanks or didn't contain tanks. After the training was complete, they tested it out with pictures it hadn't seen before. The test was successful; the system found all the pictures with tanks. The researchers decided to take more pictures to verify the results. They showed the new pictures to the system and it failed miserably. After many months of analysis of the neural network, they discovered that the system wasn't learning to distinguish between pictures with tanks and without, but whether it was a cloudy or sunny day. As it turns out, all the pictures with tanks were taken on sunny days and all the pictures without were taken on cloudy days. The moral of the story is, while neural networks are very good at discovering patterns, they may not be looking at the right data points. You need to have some feel for what the model should be focused on in order to detect fraud. To avoid these issues, pre-process your data prior to feeding it into the neural network.

Another issue you can run into is overtraining. When overtraining occurs in a neural network, the system goes from making generalizations about the data to rote memorization of patterns. Although there are clues when you cross that line, these data points will be hard for you to spot. Additionally, neural networks tend to train in batches; your model will always be lagging by some amount of time.

Deterministic Rules

Deterministic rules are just that, fixed sets of rules are designed to catch fraud. These systems are built using enterprise security managers, sometimes referred to as ESM or SIM systems. These systems can parse large numbers of data feeds, and they can apply static rules and correlate various data. Deterministic rules work well initially and are relatively easy to set up, but their effectiveness quickly deteriorates if not maintained. Any deterministic rule you put in place will be probed and worked around; assume that anything one cyber criminal finds will be disseminated to his friends. It is not unusual for deterministic rules to become ineffective within weeks. You must continuously tweak your rules to keep up with the bad guys. Be aware that some groups operate on stale knowledge and will use tactics that you saw months ago, so make sure that changes to rules still catch the prior attacks. If necessary, leave the old rule in place and create a second more advanced up-to-date rule.

Deterministic rules work best for simple logic. You can combine them with either a Bayesian system or a neural network to detect more complex attacks. For example, you may set a deterministic rule to alert you when someone attempts to transfer more than $50k to a foreign bank. A more sophisticated system might detect transfers of more than $25k to Western Union on a Friday with less than an hour until market close.

Beating Behavioral Systems

Like everything else so far, behavioral systems do have flaws. The challenge is staying under the radar. Neural networks and Bayesian statistics pose a problem for the attacker to the extent that the attacker doesn't know what "normal behavior" to mimic. Some common sense precautions can bypass these systems, just as spam still bypasses these filters. The attacker needs to blend in, keeping trade sizes in line with the victim's account. Order and equity types should match. If the target doesn't trade limit orders in the Pink Sheet market, then the attacker shouldn't use the account for that purpose. The attacker shouldn't exceed the victim's usual number of monthly trades by more than one or two standard deviations. These requirements leaves us with a trojan that launches an attack from the victim's pc, bypassing all authentication pieces, and spreading single orders across multiple accounts while staying within the amount, equity market, and order type of the victim's account. If the cyber criminal can follow these simple rules, it's likely any attack would remain under the radar of a behavioral system. The only way to detect this attack would be to have a higher level behavioral system that looks across multiple accounts and users to determine if trading in a given equity is excessive. Due to the way the markets work and the ability for news to greatly swing equity, this higher level system may not be technically feasible.

Transaction Throttling

Transaction throttling is a difficult conversation. To fight a scripted attack, you must throttle a given transaction, not only within a user's account, but across the system. Throttling is necessary because an attack could be using one or two accounts, or it can be spread across dozens of accounts. Unfortunately, no off the shelf systems or mathematical models exist to perform this task. You probably shouldn't embark down this path unless you really understand your traffic flow.

A simple model may involve breaking your users up based on how many trades they make in a given time period and forcing some sort of minimum delay based on their past behavior. This approach is not for the faint of heart. Too long a delay will anger customers; too short, and you will fall to automated attacks. Even the time of day comes into play with these systems and must be accounted for. For risk averse readers, this data could simply trip an alert and feed other systems.

Beating Transaction Throttling

Unfortunately, transaction throttling is based on modeling of large amounts of data. At the end of the day, you have a static system. Static systems fall to testing. Once properly probed and publicized, they become useless.

Historically, these systems are similar to the 3 strikes-and-you're-out style of password checking which was defeated for large user bases (AOL) by holding the password static and cycling through the user names. In this case, the attacker simply uses more than one account and executes one transaction in each. This approach avoids having to even worry about the 3 strikes.

CAPTCHA

For readers not familiar with CAPTCHA, it is an acronym for "Completely Automated Public Turing test to tell Computers and Humans Apart". The term CAPTCHA was coined by Luis von Ahn, Manuael Blum and Nicholas Hopper at Carnegie Mellon University in 2000. Discussion of an automated challenge-response test appears as early as 1996, in a manuscript written by Moni Naor.[80] CAPTCHA is a simple human-solvable challenge-response test used to determine if the user on the other end is a computer or human. Most readers are familiar with the distorted set of letters or numbers on a distorted background that appear

80. Naor, M., "Verification of a human in the loop, or Identification via the Turing Test." Manuscript, Weizmann Institute of Science, 1996. http://www.wisdom.weizmann.ac.il/#naor/PAPERS/human.ps.

with email accounts, newsletters, or blogs (Figure 14-9).

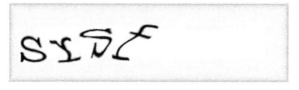

Figure 14-9 EZ-Gimpy CAPTCHA

CAPTCHA is used because it is difficult for computers to solve in a reasonable amount of time. It's an excellent system to stop scripted or automated attacks. CAPTCHA is not an authentication system, but it can help defeat scripted attacks with minimal inconvenience to the user. As the horsepower of desktop systems has increased, CAPTCHA systems have been defeated using pure brute force. This struggle has forced CAPTCHA systems to evolve over time. No matter how complex CAPTCHA gets, however, it's possible to solve any CAPTCHA by thinking out of the box and using creative ideas. The ideas presented in the next section are intended to help you understand your opponent and possible workarounds. Some of these techniques and methods can also defeat mechanisms other than CAPTCHA.

CAPTCHA certainly has its place. Some users have difficulty identifying the characters, so it is best utilized in situations where time is not an issue. The best place to use a system like this is any online form. Remember that flooding any part of your system with CAPTCHAs can have far reaching impacts that may not be immediately evident.

Beating CAPTCHA

One approach to beating CAPTCHA involves relaying the CAPTCHA challenges back to human operators for solving. While this may solution may appear costly, services such as the Amazon Mechanical Turk[81] require only micro-payments for each solution, allowing a cyber criminal to solve the problem at a relatively inexpensive cost. This method was used by spammers as early as October of 2006. Today, ads on the underground for human CAPTCHA solvers offer a starting pay of $3 per day.[82]

Alternatively, the cyber criminal could copy the CAPTCHA to a site owned by the cyber criminal. As long as the site has significant traffic, the CAPTCHA challenge space will be solved in a reasonable amount of time. Cyber criminals that use this method put the CAPTCHA on free pornographic sites, with no shortage of eager solvers. An example of this approach occurred around Halloween of 2007. A virus installed an icon of a woman. When clicked, the icon would display a larger version of the picture with the promise that the

81. Amazon Mechanical Turk. http://www.mturk.com/mturk/welcome.
82. Leydon, John. "Russian serfs paid $3 a day to break CAPTCHAs." The Register. http://www.theregister.co.uk/2008/03/14/captcha_serfs/.

woman would remove an article of clothing for each solved CAPTCHA. The CAPTCHAs solved by the striptease were used to sign up for free email accounts. There is no reason a system like this couldn't be employed against financial sites. Another variation would be to solve the solution in real time on the attacker's site and then relay back the challenge answer. This particular attack could be mitigated with a timeout on the source site.

The second major approach is to attack the implementation of the CAPTCHA system. Some CAPTCHA systems allow the reuse of the session id of a known CAPTCHA challenge. This flaw allows the attacker to manually answer one CAPT-CHA and reuse the same image and answer over and over, defeating the purpose of the CAPTCHA.

A variation of the direct attack would involve reusing the session id and using optical character recognition (OCR) to make multiple attempts at the solution. Other insecure implementations use a hash, such as MD5 or SHA-1, of the solution as a key passed to the client to validate the CAPTCHA. Unfortunately, most CAPTCHA challenges are small enough that the key can be cracked by a reasonably sized rainbow table.[83]

83.Oechslin, Philippe, "Making a Faster Cryptanalytic Time-Memory Trade-Off." Laboratire de Securite et de Cryptograhie (LASEC) Ecole Polytechnique Federale de Lausanne, 2003.

The third major approach is to attempt a mechanical solution to the CAPTCHA challenge. With a properly implemented OCR solution, modern computers can solve most CAPTCHAs more speedily and more accurately than humans.[84] The CAPTCHA shown in Figure 14-9 above was initially used by Yahoo. It has since been cracked.[85] According to MessageLabs, this failure rendered Yahoo responsible for approximately 89% of all spam from the major web mail providers. Yahoo later changed their CAPTCHA system.

Another successful mechanical attack surfaced against both the Yahoo and Hotmail signup systems. It shows that cyber criminals continue to seek automated solutions.[86] A more modern version of CAPTCHA (Figure 14-10), known as reCaptcha, uses two segmented words, making it difficult for a computer to OCR the text. These words are picked from a project to digitalize books. If the OCR fails on a word, it is added to the list. When a user is presented with the CAPTCHA, the system picks two words. The security system knows the answer to only one of the words.

---

84. Brains-n-Brawn Blog, "Using AI to beat CAPTCHA and post comment spam," http://www.brains-n-brawn.com/default.aspx?vDir=aicaptcha.

85. Mori, Greg, and Malic, Jitendra, "Breaking Visual CAPTCHA." University of California at Berkeley Computer Vision Group Simon Fraser University, 2003.

86. Pospisil , John. "Spammers overcome Hotmail and Yahoo CATCHA systems." Tech.Blorge.com. http://tech.blorge.com/Structure:%20/2007/07/08/spammers-overcome-hotmail-and-yahoo-captcha-systems/.

If the user answers the first one correctly, the unknown word is assumed to be correct too. This second word is then shown to other users until the system is confident of the answer. At this point, that word is known is moved into the known word list for reuse.

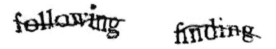

Figure 14-10 Modern CAPTCHA

Another slight variation is known as ESP-TEXT. ESP-TEXT is very similar to the CAPTCHA above except it uses pictures. The user is asked to identify a word or phrase in the picture. A sample is shown below (Figure 14-11)

Type a word or string of characters appearing in the picture

BBB ONLINE
RELIABILITY
PROGRAM

Enter

Figure 14-11 ESP-Text CAPTCHA

While ESP-TEXT is an improvement over standard CAPTCHA, further research is needed to determine if it is superior to modern CAPTCHA.

The latest spin on CAPTCHA involves the use of pictures; the most popular implementation of this update is ESP-PIX. The user is presented with four pictures and asked to select a common theme from a large dropdown (Figure 14-12).

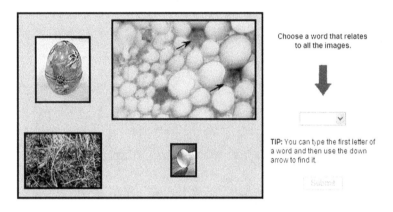

Choose a word that relates to all the images.

TIP: You can type the first letter of a word and then use the down arrow to find it.

Submit

Figure 14-12 ESP-PIX CAPTCHA

While this update may seem like a great solution, it has several drawbacks. With n choices in the dropdown, a random guess has a $1/n$ chance of success. While the odds are low, an automated system can submit multiple tries a second. Some percentage will be successful. The second issue is that the system must have a very large number of secure pictures. Even with a large corpus of pictures, the system still has significant issues. If human solvers were employed, every successful solution would give the attackers the answer to four of the pictures. If any of those pictures ever repeated, the attacker would know the answer without needing to solve the other pictures. Imagine that you have a corpus of 100,000 pictures. An attacker could see all the pictures after 25,000 views assuming the pictures are all used before being shown again. If the four pictures are chosen at random then the attacker has a 75% of knowing at least one of the pictures after seeing roughly 35,000 views.

$$[1 - (1 - P_{shown} / P_{total})^N]$$

Where

P_{shown} = Pictures shown each time displayed

P_{total} = Total number of pictures in corpus

N = The number of views

There are no large sites using this CAPTCHA variant. Consider it theoretical at this point.

Another recent attempt was to try to use simple 3-dimensional scenes for CAPTCHA. The concept is that the user would be presented with a simple 3-dimensional scene; this scene is composed of a random set of objects with various labeled attributes. The user would be asked questions such as "Which person is sitting?", "Which object is the vase?" and the like. This method fails, however, when human solvers are used. While developing computer programs to analyze 3-dimensional scenes is difficult, it shouldn't be ruled out. As computer horsepower increases, the likelihood of a machine-based solution increases.[87]

The reader must understand that the cyber criminal doesn't need to solve a given CAPTCHA every time to be successful. If he can solve even a small percentage of your CAPTCHAs, then he can achieve automation at the expense of time. Again, implement CAPTCHA as one of several layers of security controls. Make it one more roadblock that a cyber criminal must cross in order to accomplish his goal.

Fingerprint Biometrics

Fingerprint biometrics are simply mentioned because everyone thinks they will solve the problem. Although expensive and difficult to deploy, some companies may think they are appropriate for high-value clients. The system is simple enough, a user places or swipes his finger on a scanning device to authenticate. An algorithm creates a fingerprint pattern between 50 and 1000 bytes in size.

---

87. Kaplan, Michael G. "3-dimensional scenes for CAPTCHA." http://spamfizzle.com/CAPTCHA.aspx.

Beating Fingerprint Biometrics

You may have read about people beating these systems with gummi worms and the like; however those attacks involved the attacker being physically present. The cyber criminal must attack these systems remotely. The attack, like other systems, is quite easy. At some point, a pattern is created and stored; if the attacker can get to that pattern he can replay it. Even if the pattern is stored in a removable device, at some point some data must leave the device to give a match/no match signal. The cyber criminal has multiple places to hook this system and lift this pattern using the same techniques as traditional keylogger.[88] If you recall the diagram at the start of Chapter 6, all you have really done is replaced the keyboard with a fingerprint scanner. Data still must move and make its way to the destination web server, and as we have seen time and time again, that leaves them open to compromise and manipulation.

Voice Recognition

Voice recognition is great for authenticating users into an IVR system, since it allows you to get rid of PINs for access. Typically in an IVR system a user will enter his account number and speak a

88. Jackson Higgins, Kelly. "Black Hat Researcher Hacks Biometric System." Dark Reading, March 31, 2008. http://www.darkreading.com/document.asp?doc_id=149661&WT.svl=news2_1.

pass-phrase. A voice recognition system then uses various vocal characteristics to validate the user's identity. Unfortunately, you will likely run into two main issues. First, getting your users to enroll is difficult, any account not enrolled leaves valuable accounts open to access by a cyber criminal via the IVR system. Additionally, recognition of the user could be greatly impacted by background noise, and in this day and age of cell phones, it's a likely scenario. Currently, it is unclear if the technology can actually recognize the user's voice or if it is just recognizing the pronunciation of the pass-phrase. This vulnerability has been under considerable investigation by various groups attempting to improve the accuracy of the systems. When investigating these systems, make sure you pay attention to the false positive and false negative rates. Also be sure to test the system's resistance to a recorded sample of the user's voice, as the user may fall for a vishing attempt one day.

Terms

ActiveX – A technology developed by Microsoft. This technology adds browser functionality similar to Java applets.

FFIEC –Federal Financial Institutions Examination Council. The FFIEC is a formal interagency body empowered to prescribe uniform principles, standards, and report forms for the federal examination of financial institutions by the Board of Governors of the Federal Reserve System, the Federal Deposit Insurance Corporation, the National Credit Union Administration, the Office of the Comptroller of the Currency, and the Office of Thrift Supervision. The FFIEC makes recommendations to promote uniformity in the supervision of financial institutions.[89]

Certificate Authority – A company or individual responsible for the issuance and management of digital certificates used in public key systems.

Hash – A hash function takes a piece of data of any length and outputs a fixed length string. This string, called a hash, is a

---

89. Federal Financial Institutions Examination Council (FFIEC). http://www.ffiec.gov.

digital fingerprint of the original data. The role of the hash is to prove that the data has not been tampered with.

Java – An object-oriented programming language, similar to C++, developed by Sun Microsystems. Java is designed to be portable across operating systems.

MD5- Message Digest 5. MD5 is a one-way hash function created in 1991 by Professor Ronald Rivest. The algorithm outputs a 128-bit fingerprint.

Micro-payments – Financial transactions, usually under $3.00, that occur on the Internet. These small value transactions do not warrant the use of a credit card payment due to the high cost to process the transaction.

OCR – Optical Character Recognition. OCR is the automated scanning and conversion of printed text into machine readable text.

PDA – Personal Digital Assistant. A PDA is a handheld device that acts as a personal organizer and often provides connectivity to e-mail and the Internet.

Rainbow Table – A pre-calculated table that trades time for memory, used to speed

up a process. Typically used for breaking hash tables.

Replay Attack – An attack on a system that
occurs by recording and replaying a previously sent valid message.

SHA-1 – Secure Hash Algorithm. SHA-1 is one
of the five cryptographic hash functions
designed by the NSA. The algorithm
outputs a 160-bit fingerprint. SHA-2 is
often used to refer to the other SHA
functions, which are labeled based on
the length of the fingerprint they output.
They consist of SHA-224, SHA-256,
SHA-384 and SHA-512.

SMS – Short Message Service. SMS is a service
designed for sending messages of up to
160 characters to mobile devices.

Token – In the case of enhanced authentication
systems, a token is a unique identifier
that is generated and sent from the
server to the client to identify the computer. A token is usually stored in a
cookie or a Flash object.

CHAPTER 15 Client-Side Countermeasures

The supreme end of education is expert discernment in all things--the power to tell the good from the bad, the genuine from the counterfeit, and to prefer the good and the genuine to the bad and the counterfeit.

- Samuel Johnson

Prevention is the most important piece of any countermeasure; the client side is all about prevention. If you can prevent an infection or portion of infections, your job is much easier. You don't have to fix computers that haven't been exploited. Once malware is installed, it can be so difficult to remove that a complete rebuild of the infected system is the only solution.

Your company should have a strategy in place to deploy some sort of prevention tool to your customers, free of charge. The cost benefit for such a distribution can't be justified by looking solely at losses. Still, it makes sense, and I will explain why.

Offering all of your customers some sort of free preventative tool appears to make sense. Your company offers a free tool and losses from fraud go down. You and your customer both win. Under certain circumstances, the winner may not be as clear. You will run into cost justification issues for any tools with recurring subscriptions. A subset of your client base will either already own the tool, or a competitor's tool, and will be paying for a subscription. As soon as you market your free offering, a percentage of your customer base will migrate to your offering because it is free. Ninety plus percent of your clients that already own the tool will switch to you. A smaller subset of clients with a competitor's tool will also move to you. In these cases, you will need to rely on the more nebulous numbers like customer satisfaction, increased gains in subscribers due to you caring about security, and other data points.

The one recurring issue to keep in mind is that these systems, running on the client side, are subject to direct assault by the malware they are attempting to prevent. If the right piece of malware sneaks by these systems, the malware has the ability to circumvent all of the controls that you have put in place. You are also relying on your customer to set up the software correctly and maintain it, and potentially pay for updates if you are unwilling to take on the burden. It's not all doom and gloom. The free press that you receive for your initiative will offset at least a portion of your investment.

Anti-Virus Systems

Recent studies have shown that roughly 85% of users believe they have anti-virus software running on their computers. In reality, 87% of users' computers have anti-virus software installed. Only 51% of those computers, however, have a functional anti-virus program, meaning the software is current, running, and checking for recent virus patterns. There hasn't been any notable study on why users install anti-virus software but then don't update it. The author believes there are two core issues. First, many new computers come preinstalled with a trial version of an anti-virus application. It's likely the user activated this trial and didn't want to pay for a subscription. Second, the user may not understand that an update service is required for full protection. Many anti-virus products will continue to run without an update. The user may think his computer is protected without the subscription. Based on some surveys, the latter may be closer to the truth.

Anti-virus software should impact your loss enough to pay for itself, though that may not always be the case. Users with active anti-virus software, particularly software by the same vendor, will switch to your free offering as their subscriptions expire, typically within one year. These users actually become a burden to your company, as they are likely not impacting your loss numbers. You need to find a way to reach the scores of users with outdated or nonexistent anti-virus defenses at the same time as you pick up the tab for already protected users.

Anti-virus has a certain published effectiveness rate. This number is not applicable to you. You need to understand what type of malware is being targeted at your users. Then you need to figure out the effectiveness of your chosen anti-virus product.

By offering free anti-virus software, you are creating another risk. You are creating an anti-virus monoculture. In other words, you are reducing the burden of the cyber criminals. They have to circumvent only a single anti-virus product to infiltrate a large percentage of your customer base.

It is absolutely critical that you monitor with the threats to your users. Form a close partnership with your vendor so that you can quickly get pattern updates for any malware specifically targeting your users.

All of these factors add up to an extremely difficult analysis. The return on investment (ROI) will not become positive unless you can convince only users with no functional anti-virus products to install it, or add marketing value and other factors into the equation.

Anti-virus systems are interesting in the sense that the problem they are trying to solve and the method required to solve it directly conflicts with the primary requirements of the product. An anti-virus product attempts to accurately identify an infection in a file while minimizing latency and CPU load. These two requirements are diametrically opposed. For an anti-virus system to identify an infection, it needs to completely analyze every byte of a given executable, converting it into some sort of high level pseudocode. By doing this work, you reduce the number of patterns you may need for a given piece of code. If in my malware I need to do a loop, and in that loop execute a specific function, there are several methods typically available to me. The exact method I choose is a matter of taste more than anything else. However, if I use two different methods to code my loop and execute my function, I have created two completely different programs, with different anti-virus signatures. With a proper analysis tool, the pseudocode output for any type of loop looks identical. A single pattern could identify the code. The mandate to minimize latency and CPU load, makes it impossible to create an anti-virus system like this example, even with the fastest processors available. These secondary requirements continue to reduce the effectiveness of modern anti-virus systems.

Most anti-virus systems rely on two methods to detect a virus: pattern matching and heuristics.

Pattern matching is very straightforward. Anti-virus vendors are alerted to a virus either by submission or via a set of proprietary honeypots. They analyze the newly discovered virus, looking for unique sections of code that allow the manufacturer to create a signature for the malicious program. The vendor creates a pattern to detect and clean the malware. The pattern is then distributed to their customers. The average vendor releases a pattern anywhere from a few hours to a few days after detection.

To meet the requirements of reducing latency and CPU load, an anti-virus product cannot scan entire file for a suspicious pattern. Most anti-virus products look at the first few kilobytes of a file, the last few kilobytes or a mix of the two for speed.

The major problem with pattern creation is the time it takes to get a sample of a virus coupled with the sheer volume of viruses in the wild. Malware writers have binders and packers that allow them to mutate their virus in minutes. A binder is a program that allows you to combine two executables to form a new combined executable. This combination offsets the malware code so that the anti-virus signatures do not match. Some of the better binders available on the Internet are Infector v2, Exe-Maker, Exe-Joiner, Trojan Man, Elitewrap and TOP. A packer, also known as a compressor, is another way to bypass detection. The packer simply compresses the malware so that the anti-virus signatures do not match. Some of the better packers include Shrinker, PKlite, AS-pack, Petite, and WWpack.

Code obfuscation, also known as morphing, is another difficult issue for pattern based anti-virus systems. Nondeterministic transformations, such as inserting NOP instructions, code transposition and register reassignment make signature detection useless. Code obfuscation also makes malware analysis more difficult. Some of the better code obfuscators include EXECryptor, Mistfall, and Burneye. Polymorphic malware is very similar, in that it encrypts itself and uses a code obfuscation system to constantly change its signature.

Code conversion is also another way to hide from pattern based anti-virus systems. Programs like the exe2vbs converter can take any executable and hide it inside a VBS script. This system works because the code conversion changes the virus signature.

The situation is becoming worse for anti-virus vendors. Virus writers can keep distributions limited. Malware distributions sites have begun repacking each individual piece of malware that gets distributed, making unique signatures for each deployed piece. In either of these cases the anti-virus vendor will never be able to collect all of the samples of a given virus strain. As mutation engines become more evolved, it's questionable whether an effective set of patterns could ever be developed to match all possible mutations.

Unfortunately, current anti-virus architectures are reactive. If malware is able to maintain a low profile, infecting fewer than 100,000 computers, then it will likely never be detected by the vendor's honeypots or submitted by an end-user. Even if it was feasible to capture every variant, it is financially infeasible to create, test and distribute such a large number of signatures. The end result is a piece of malware that can stay installed and active on a person's computer for months or even years. How bad is detection of malware today? During one study, anti-virus products failed to detect over 70%+ of malware.

To be fair to the anti-virus companies, many of these malware infections were variants of a family of viruses specifically designed to evade detection.

To understand why current anti-virus method-ologies fail, consider the following analogy. Imagine you need to connect two computers together over one single port through a firewall. Is it easier to black list ports and IP addresses as attacks hit you? Or is it easier to just white list the two computers and the single port they need? With anti-virus systems, the number of patterns to blacklist can grow large, almost infinite. Looking in the other direction, the number of executables a user or system uses is finite. It makes more sense for anti-virus vendors to move away from the question of, "Is this file bad?" to "Is this file good?" Of course there will be exceptions, and users will need to be technically savvy about what they allow to run. For the population at large that just turns on their PCs and goes, a white listing system may offer superior protection.

Symantec a large player in the anti-virus space, estimates that there is one new virus released to the Windows platform every four hours. Remember, that's *new* viruses. This figure does not account for all the mutations that may spawn from that one new piece of code. The Yankee Group indicated that there has been an explosion in the number of malware variants, with over 220,000 unique variants in 2007 alone, a ten fold increase in five years.[90] AV-Test, a company that tests anti-

90. Jaquith, Andrew. "Anti-Virus is Dead; Long Live Anti-Malware." The Yankee Group. http://www.yankeegroup.com/ResearchDocument.do?id=15059.

virus products, claims that in 2007 they saw an estimated 5.49 million unique samples of malware, compared to 973,606 they saw the prior year. It doesn't matter who has the number right. Obviously, malware is likely mutating at a pace far greater than anyone can maintain.

To be truly effective, anti-virus vendors would need to issue updates as frequently as every 2.4 minutes to keep up with the variants. Doing so would create a denial of service attack against the anti-virus vendor's update servers. The anti-virus industry will ultimately be forced to a continuous stream of updates in order to keep up. Even with a massive amount of effort, anti-virus will continue weaken.

Given the problems with signature based technology, it's easy to see why some sort of high level pseudocode conversion system could be the only savior of the anti-virus industry.

Of course, anti-virus vendors were able to foresee all of these events. Their solution was heuristics. Heuristic methods are nothing new; anti-virus vendors incorporated them into their products years ago. Heuristics is a misnomer. What anti-virus vendors are creating is dynamic pattern systems. Instead of looking at a static signature, they may look for several features that flag a piece of code as malware.

Heuristics worked very well initially, but became useless once the malware writers moved to packing and encrypting their code. At the beginning of 2007, anti-virus heuristics could identify 40%-50% of malware. By the end of 2007, that number had dropped to 20%-30%.[91] Ultimately, vendors fell back to static signatures for most of their detection.[92] Interestingly, a similar evolutionary pattern was seen with Bayesian spam detection.

Anti-Trojan Systems

Anti-trojan software is marketed as a product similar to anti-virus software. Anti-trojan software usually utilizes behavior analysis to detect malware. This software actually has more in common with host-based intrusion prevention systems (HIPS) than anti-virus software though its behavioral analysis may sometimes be complemented by dynamic patterns, depending on the manufacturer.

The major benefit of anti-trojan systems is that they shore up existing anti-virus solutions on the user's computer. Testing has shown that a typical anti-trojan system can detect 50%-80% of trojans. When combined with an anti-virus system, anti-

91. Heise Security. "Antivirus protection worse than a year ago." Heise Security. http://www.heise?security.co.uk/news/100900.

92. Szor, Peter, The Art of Computer Virus Research and Defense, Symantec Press, 2005.

trojan systems can pick up about 40%-60% of what typical anti-virus systems miss. The reason for this lower number is due to the fact that there is sometimes an overlap in detection.

To implement an anti-trojan system, a user installs a fat client product on his computer. The anti-trojan system then enumerates the processes on the computer and uses a combination of risk scoring and white listing to determine if a specific process is malware or not. To understand how some of these protections work, you must understand what trojans typically attack.

Process termination is one of the most basic tools in a cyber criminal's toolkit. If a trojan can terminate a piece of security software, he renders it useless. To terminate a process a trojan simply acquires the SeDebugPrivilege, which grants a process permission to terminate other processes. The trojan then calls the TerminateProcess function in the kernel32.dll library, actually terminating the target process. There is no way to detect or counter this termination command without using some form of driver based solution. Security software vendors rarely use this type of solution due to their complexity.

Process suspension is similar to process termination, except that the trojan attempts to suspend all of the threads associated with the security software's running process. This approach leaves the security program resident in memory, but inactive, frozen, and completely useless.

Code modification is a more advanced tool. It works by simply modifying running code in memory. Code modification allows the attacker to change the intended behavior of the code to suit his needs. The trojan simply needs write access to the memory space of the security software's process.

```
004016C8   74 21         JE SHORT 004016EB    Jumps to "blocked"
004016CA   48            DEC EAX
004016CB   74 17         JE SHORT 004016E4    Jumps to
                                              "permitted"
004016CD   51            PUSH ECX
004016CE   4A            DEC EDX
004016CF   68 E0614300   PUSH 004361E0
004016D4   52            PUSH EDX
004016D5   56            PUSH ESI
004016D6   E8 ACB20100   CALL 00410987
```

Figure 15-1 Inside the Firewall

Above is a code snippet from an actual firewall product (Figure 15-1). This code is executed when a firewall rule is triggered. The code then determines if the firewall should deny the traffic, or permit it based on the rule. Unfortunately, it is simple for a cyber criminal to make one minor change to this code as it runs. He simply copies the line that permits traffic, and pastes it over the line that blocks, as shown below (Figure 15-2).

004016C8	74 21	JE SHORT 004016E4	Jumps to "permitted"
004016CA	48	DEC EAX	
004016CB	74 17	JE SHORT 004016E4	Jumps to "permitted"
004016CD	51	PUSH ECX	
004016CE	4A	DEC EDX	
004016CF	68 E0614300	PUSH 004361E0	
004016D4	52	PUSH EDX	
004016D5	56	PUSH ESI	
004016D6	E8 ACB20100	CALL 0041C987	

Figure 15-2 Disabling the Firewall

The firewall now allows all traffic through, though to the user it appears fully functional. Without some form of port scan, the user would never even know this attack occurred. Of course, an attack like this is much more complex than simple process termination. It requires detailed knowledge of the target software, such as by decompiling a copy of the software.

Code injection, which we explored in earlier chapters, is a similar idea with a different implementation. Trojans inject code or a dll into another process for one of two reasons. The first reason is so that the trojan can run code under the pretext of another process. The infected process, rather than the trojan, appears to be performing actions. For example, a trojan could inject code into the web browser. The web browser is normally trusted by the firewall. When the trojan attempts to move data out, the data appears to be coming from the browser, and is allowed through the firewall. The second reason to inject code is so that the trojan can modify the code in the injected process. Once injected, the trojan can change the behavior of existing code as well as adding any new code. Simply enabling the Data Execution Protection (DEP) system in Microsoft Windows can very effectively mitigate a large portion of traditional code injection attacks.[93]

A few key characteristics determine the risk score for anti-trojan applications. We will explore some of them, along with possible workarounds for the cyber criminal. This list is not comprehensive; however it is a minimal list of requirements for an effective system.

Some parts that go into a risk score:

Characteristic: Is the executable registered as a system service and yet it is hidden from the user?

Idea: This is highly suspicious behavior for any program and could be a tell tale sign that this is a root-kit.

93. Riley, Ryan, Jiang, Xuxian, and Xu, Dongyan, "An Architectural Approach to Preventing Code Injection Attacks." Purdue, 2007. http://friends.cs.purdue.edu/pubs/dsn07-codeinj.pdf.

Workaround: Hidden services should typically be avoided by cyber criminals, for the most part their targets are not savvy enough to identify an executable that shouldn't be on the system.

Characteristic: Is the executable packed with a suspicious packer?

Idea: Some executables are packed in order to reduce the size of the installation. Many pieces of malware pack their code in order to evade detection by a signature based mechanism.

Workaround: Most signature based systems do not completely scan a file so it's often unnecessary to pack. The cyber criminals will likely move toward morphing code that can pad the head and tail of their code. A more advance trick would be to shuffle modules around along with padding the head and tail of each module. For the short time, packing is still an efficient evasion technique and will likely continue for some time to come.

Characteristic: Was the executable installed via IM, email or a browser?

Idea: These are the three biggest holes for malware to enter a system. Any code launching from one of these sources is immediately suspect.

Workaround: It may be possible to create a non-threatening installer that installs the malicious code.

There are dozens of others. How ever the characteristics typically revolve around what a specific process is (hidden, questionable name, etc) or what it does (writes to the network, hooks another process, etc). While definitely a challenge it should be possible to workaround a significant number so that the system will not detect the malware.

Based on this author's field testing, good anti-trojan systems can detect approximately 50% of malware. While this average may seem extremely bad, when combined with an anti-virus product, this type of system helps fill the gaps left by anti-virus products that don't yet have a pattern for a given piece of malware.

Anti-spam Systems

Anti-spam systems are designed with one goal in mind. Rid the user of unsolicited bulk email. When it comes to fraud, these systems have a slightly different purpose. The function of the anti-spam system is to prevent forged emails that appear to be coming from legitimate sources. By preventing these emails, the user is less likely to open an email that may install malicious code, steal their credentials, or redirect them to a phishing site.

The anti-spam market tends to fare much worse than the anti-virus market. Most of these issues are due to the fact that there is so much spam these days, that legitimate email has become the proverbial "needle in the haystack". In 2003, spam surpassed legitimate mail, representing over 50% of all email. At the end of 2007, spam had become over 95% of all email (Figure 15-3).

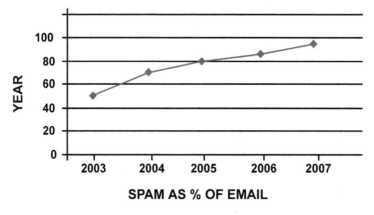

Figure 15-3 Spam as a Percent of Total Email by Year

Beating Anti-Spam Systems

Much has been written about the spam industry and how to combat spam. Most of it is out-of-scope for this book. Spam *does* play a role in pump-and-dump scams, so in this section we will briefly touch on the evolution of stock spam.

Initially, stock spam consisted of nothing more than text messages touting a specific security. Spam filters quickly caught on to these messages, and the spam arms race began. Early attempts to bypass spam past filters involved appending random characters to the subject header and adding book passages to the body text. Many of these techniques are still in use today, used in combined with other advances, to increase the likelihood of delivery.

The basic text spam later evolved into an image based spam message to bypass text based filters. As anti-spam systems developed optical character recognition capabilities (OCR), the spammers deployed basic counter measures, such as the low-contrast colors and misaligned text (Figure 15-4). This is the exact CAPTCHA problem in reverse, no more and no less.

```
      Takes Investors For Second Climb! UP
40%.

Score One Inc. (      )
$0.42 UP 40%

      continues another huge climb this week
after hot news was released Friday.
                    .us has released        as
featured StockWatch. This one is still
cooking. Go read the news and get on
Tuesday!
```

Figure 15-4 Attempt to Defeat OCR Anti-Spam Systems

Unfortunately, these anti-spam filter counter-measures reduced the believability and credibility of the message, both necessary to pump up a security. The search was on for a solution to the problem. The career spammers needed a way to bypass text and images scanners, while still placing a convincing message in front of the victim. The more believable the image, the more likely the spammer could move the stock and line his pockets.

Over time, spammers were able to fine-tune their anti-OCR capabilities by using less image distortion (Figure 15-5). Colored sprinkles and other light-color distortions in the backgrounds of these images became highly popular. These techniques were often enough to throw off even the most sophisticated anti-spam systems.

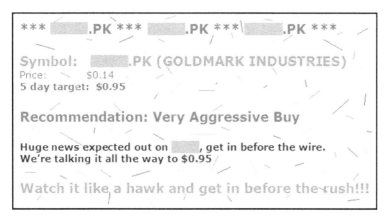

*** ___.PK *** ___.PK *** ___.PK ***

Symbol: ___.PK (GOLDMARK INDUSTRIES)
Price: $0.14
5 day target: $0.95

Recommendation: Very Aggressive Buy

Huge news expected out on ___, get in before the wire.
We're talking it all the way to $0.95

Watch it like a hawk and get in before the rush!!!

Figure 15-5 Attempt to Defeat Anti-Spam Systems with "Sprinkles"

Spammers continued their research, and what resulted was a more believable message. At this time, spammers that specialized in stock spam learned their biggest lesson. It is more important to get a believable and professional looking message into the hands of the victims than to get sheer quantity of messages out. Targeting victims is more important than mass mail the world. Fewer believable messages getting past filters and to high quality targets is more desirable and profitable than sending messages to hundreds of millions of users.

The use of Adobe portable document format (PDF) attachments (figure 35) looked like it may be the answer. This technique quickly became the distribution method of choice. The spammers achieved what they needed, a very professional looking message that could have come from an investing firm. Spammers have been successful getting these past anti-spam systems using a number of techniques.

Figure 15-6 A PDF Stock Spam Attachment

Within months, companies started blocking emails containing PDF attachments, which partially DOSed their own workforce. It didn't take long for the spammers to change their attack. The new format of choice? Microsoft Excel's xls format. Fortunately, this threat was quickly dispatched, as .xls is only rarely emailed outside of companies.

Anti-Exploit Systems

Anti-exploit tools are an up and coming trend, LinkScanner by Exploit Prevention Labs is one of the few tools in this space. The company looked at the anti-virus market and realized there is an infinite number of virus mutation variations in a given period of time. The solution was to look at how these viruses were getting inside and onto machines. Exploit Prevention Labs built an exploit detector. Exploits tend to be a relatively short list. Due to the complexity of finding an exploit and using it, virus writers often use the same exploit over. LinkScanner looks at web sites in real time to determine if there is any exploit code on the web site, warning the user if hostile code is present. In addition to pattern based functionality, the product is further shored up with heuristics.

Other companies, like McAfee, are attempting to enter this space with products such as McAfee SiteAdvisor. SiteAdvisor must visit a web site, which then updates a central database. The data contained in the database may be extremely stale. In this day and age, it's not out of the question that an attacker's site may be up for a few days, then gone, leaving SiteAdvisor with no information about the site. It's likely that this tool will receive some sort of real-time scan capability. It's not clear, however, that SiteAdvisor is scanning for exploits. It's more likely that it compares any downloads against McAfee's anti-virus product, potentially missing quite a bit.

Microsoft has been seen also in this market space with the Strider HoneyMonkey project which attempts to detect and analyze web sites hosting malicious code.

While these technologies are very promising, consumer inability to understand the subtle differences between an anti-virus program, anti-trojan program and an anti-exploit program may prevent wide scale adoption. These types of tools may see a surge in customers if financial services companies start giving away this software or if search engines start using the technology to vet sites prior to serving them up in results pages.

Keyboard Monitors

Inline keyboard/mouse monitors are one of the current unsolved issues in the computer world. Not only do PS/2 and USB hardware key loggers exist, but there are now even laptop key loggers available on the market.[94]

However there are two likely future directions available to correct the issue.

The likely winner of this horse race would be a secure keyboard. Conceptually, the keyboard would work the same as a normal keyboard. A

---

94. keycatcher.com. http://www.keycatcher.com.

small encryption chip placed inside the keyboard that would work with a secure keyboard driver in the computer. Security keys could be negotiated and all data could be transmitted, in encrypted form, across the wire. We can use this system to help deter snatching of the keystrokes by allowing an application to request a secure channel to the keyboard. This capability would provide fingertip to application security, not only eliminating the possibility of credential theft; it would prevent transaction injection via the keyboard buffer. If you refer back to figure 12, a properly implemented solution could eliminate the issue from the keyboard all the way to the browser.

This technology does exist. Microcontrollers that can support a secure keyboard are already in most good keyboards. Unfortunately, no one has leveraged this technology, even though it can be enabled by simply flashing a chip and writing a driver. The keyboard would require a mechanism to allow applications to connect securely to the keyboard.

The second possibility would be a detection type system. All inline devices draw power from the same wires the keyboards use. A sensitive system could detect the current drain. Simply flashing a light, or popping up information on the screen, would alert the user. Of course, the design would have to plan for malicious users attempting to disable the alert mechanism. This option may be cost prohibitive, but may be of interest to certain government agencies.

Ideally, the computer industry will get to the point where not only keystrokes are secure all the way into applications, but the keyboard itself is paired to the computer at setup. This step would prevent cyber criminals from replacing a user's keyboard with one containing built-in key logging, unfortunately this approach essentially opposes Plug-and-Play technology.

Anti-Rootkit Tools

Rootkits are often confused with malware. A rootkit is a method designed to hide a piece of malware. A rootkit can be paired up with just about any piece of malware. Removal of a rootkit presents a challenge, as rootkit developers are finding new ways to hide from users and forensic tools.

Fortunately, Rootkits are still in their infancy, and are currently suffering from the same issues as early viruses. Rootkits will follow a similar evolution, including adding polymorphism capabilities. Be aware that research is advancing quickly. Theoretical work has been done around virtual memory subversion in Windows. This stealth technique can fool in-memory scanners by presenting a false view of what's in memory. This technique can also fool scanners that look for hooks. Once these techniques become mainstream, detecting and removing a rootkit will be that much harder.

Rootkit categories

There are currently five major categories of rootkit. We will briefly explain each one before going into possible countermeasures.

The firmware rootkit utilizes a portion of a device's firmware to hold the rootkit. This approach is often very effective, since firmware is loaded into very low level memory. Most tools also do not check firmware for changes. Firmware, however, varies a lot. No known rootkits have used this method as of the writing of this book.[95,96] Targeted attacks of this sort will likely never be found.

The virtual machine based rootkit, or VMBR, is currently the lowest level rootkit seen in the wild. This type of rootkit modifies the boot sequence and loads itself first. It then continues the original boot sequence, loading the operating system into a virtual machine. The rootkit can run undetected and intercept any hardware call to the operating system. A proof of concept rootkit utilizing this

---

95. Heasman , John, "Implementing and Detecting an ACPI Rootkit," Blackhat Federal, Washington, DC, 2006.

96. Heasman , John, "Implementing and Detecting a PCI Rootkit." NGS-Software, November 15, 2006.

method was developed jointly by Microsoft and the University of Michigan.[97]

The kernel level rootkit operates by adding additional code to the operating system or by replacing a portion of kernel code to hide a piece of malware. Typically, the new code is added via a device driver in Microsoft Windows or by a loadable kernel module in Linux.

Library level rootkits are also commonly referred to as patch or hook rootkits. This category of rootkits replaces system calls with code that helps conceal the malware.

Application level rootkits are the last category. These rootkits replace a program's code with malware infected versions. They preserve the function of the original application; however they inject additional functions for use by the cyber criminal.

Rootkit Detection Methods

The implementation of the various categories of rootkit varies greatly. The skill set required to implement them varies even more so. Various detection methods will typically work against one

---

97. King, Samuel T., Chen, Peter M., Wang, Yi-Min, Verbowski, Chad ,Wang, Helen J., and Lorch, Jacob R., "SubVirt: Implementing malware with virtual machines." University of Michigan, 2007. http://www.eecs.umich.edu/~pmchen/papers/king06.pdf.

or more categories. There are four major rootkit detection methods:

Signature based systems work basically the same as anti-virus products. Signatures are produced by sampling rootkits; these signatures are then distributed via pattern updates to the rootkit detection product. While signature based systems are today extremely accurate, they will soon suffer from the same issues that plague the anti-virus products discussed earlier in this chapter. They cannot, for example, detect unknown rootkits, rootkits for which a signature does not exist, code that has been intentionally obfuscated, and modern rootkits that modify memory rather than files on the hard drive. As rootkits evolve and add polymorphism, these types of systems will ultimately fail. When combined with another method, you will have the best of both worlds.

The second method is integrity checking, found in products such as TripWire. Integrity checking detects unauthorized changes to system files or loaded OS components in RAM (memory). It does so by creating an initial baseline database containing hashes, often multiple hashes, of each known good file. TripWire then periodically calculates and compares the hashes against the trusted baseline, looking for changes. These types of file system integrity checks are completely ineffective against rootkits that make their changes to memory.

The third method is behavior detection, found in products such as Primary Response SafeConnect by Sana Security, PatchFinder by Joanna Rutkowska, and VICE by Jamie Butler. Behavior detection is likely to be the future direction of most companies. The more advanced detection systems that look for diverting execution paths, by detecting hooks, or by detecting the alterations in the number, order or frequency of system calls, tend to suffer from high rates of false positives. The average computer user would probably not have the training to accurately screen out the false alerts. The high false positive rate may be overcome when combined with other techniques, such as whitelisting, signature based detection, and others.

Diff Based detection (Microsoft Strider Ghost-Buster, SysInternals Rootkit Revealer, F-Secure Blacklight) works similarly to integrity checking; however it doesn't require an initial baseline. These tools work by comparing the system's view of an object to what appears in storage. The concept is that a rootkit, to be persistent, must save itself to permanent storage. At the same time, the rootkit must hide itself from the system. If you look at the system view and compare it to the raw entries on disk, they should match. If they don't, the difference indicates the presence of a rootkit.

Sandboxing/Virtualization

Sandboxing and virtualization are interesting technologies that are common only inside the corporate arena. The concept is that your browser runs virtualized. The client's personal computer can be protected since the browser is running within an isolated area within your system. At the end of browsing the Internet, the client simply closes out his sandbox or virtual computer. Any malware that may have been installed in the virtualized environment is wiped clean. Virtualization comes in a few flavors. Some virtualization products are designed to sandbox a single application, other products, such as VMware or Virtual PC, emulate an entire PC. A program that virtualizes just an application may be less secure than one that virtualizes the entire computer; the difference depends more on the skill of the development team than anything else.

Several companies have application virtualization products designed specifically to protect clients while surfing the Internet. The most popular companies include: BufferZone, GreenBorder, recently acquired by Google, SandBoxie, and ShadowSurfer. These products provide varying degrees of protection and options.

A sandbox or virtualization product should be able to protect several key areas of your system. Protection of the host machine when surfing drive-by install sites is critical. While all virtualization products should do this, performance shortcuts often lead to compromised security. The virtualized application must protect the host file system, otherwise malware may be saved to the host computer. Again, this goal should be straightforward. Some virtualized products, however try to minimize compatibility issues by removing features, causing huge security holes. The sandboxed application must also segregate itself from raw memory. If a sandboxed piece of malware can read and write raw memory, the malware can infect the host system. Sandboxed application data must also be kept separate from key pieces of information about the host. If a sandboxed piece of malware can gather information about the host, then the attacker is in a much stronger position to infect that computer. With the proper information, an attacker can directly assault the sandbox itself. As with other security software, protect the sandbox software from termination. If an attacker is able to terminate the sandbox process, then the protection the sandbox provides to the host is lost. Additionally, termination of the sandbox could cause the loss of forensic data such as history files, book mark changes, etc.

Like all software, sandboxes and virtualization products have security flaws. These flaws may allow an attacker to infect the personal computer. When used for security, virtualization products make a huge and unwarranted assumption; the client's personal computer is clean of any malware. If malware exists on the personal computer, the game is over before it began. The only way to truly ensure that a computer remains clean is to fully configure a computer, apply the best sandbox/virtualization tool out there, and set it to delete any information when it's closed. Short of such extreme measures, it's unlikely this solution can effectively make a difference. Virtualization may be able to prevent a portion of your users from getting infected, but for those with malware already deeply imbedded, recovery and return to a safe environment is an impossible goal without a complete rebuild of the system.

Custom Browsers

A custom browser is an application that provides the functionality of a browser but embeds additional technology based on the needs of the client. These systems can embed mutual authentication, public key encryption and digital signatures. The logic behind creating these systems is that the major browsers on the market have security flaws that allow cyber criminals to attack you. While the major browsers certainly are flawed, it's unlikely that another company can do much better. These custom browsers also attempt to increase security by starting at the application layer and going to the web server. They completely ignore issues prior to the application tier. Since custom browsers skip those layers, the cyber criminal has plenty of options, including session take-over, session ridding, and credential theft. At the end of the day, custom browsers aren't much better than Internet Explorer or Firefox with a VPN tunnel.

On top of the standard set of problems, partnering with a company to provide this technology ties you to that company for the foreseeable future. If new technology comes out, it may not be supported. If you make this technology mandatory, you will have removed the flexibility that off the shelf browsers provide. For example, it's unlikely that clients at their place of business will be able to download and install your custom browser, nor will kiosk users, etc.

Beating Custom Browsers

Beating the custom browsers doesn't take much work. Once the bad guy has compromised the local machine, he can steal all the information he needs to replicate the user's installation some place else. Once the installation is replicated, the technology is busted. Additionally, if auto-authentication isn't embedded in the browser, outright credential theft is always an option for the resourceful thief.

Just because there aren't a lot of custom browsers out there, don't assume that no one will target you. If your company is an attractive target, cyber criminals will assault the technology. Your attempt at security by obscurity will crumble.

Secure Browsers

Secure browsers are new to the market. These systems may ultimately be the protection that online companies need. Success, however, requires assistance from hardware vendors to close the remaining holes.

Secure browsers rely on one of two methods to provide security. Method one consists of inserting their own keyboard drivers. The driver passes the user's credentials, encrypted, into the secure browser. The browser could be a standalone Windows application, or it could be an ActiveX control, flash object or other technology that removes control from the browser. The secure browser then initiates a secure connection back to the web server. The second method consists of using hardware assisted virtual machines to spawn a hardware protected browser. When the browser has focus it has complete control of all system resources, preventing any malware on the computer from accessing the keystrokes. Unfortunately, hardware assisted virtual machines can only run on the latest processors from Intel and AMD.

Various secure browsers exist. Several more are on the drawing boards at various start-ups. Not all secure browsers are created equally, however. These applications need to insert their keyboard drivers at as low a level as possible in the operating system, since the one at the bottom of the stack wins. At the same time, they must be able to verify that nothing has inserted itself at a lower level. If the browser fails at either task, a programmer with better skills can inject code into their driver or insert code underneath their driver. Either way, the cyber criminal can steal all the credentials, just like a standard key logger. The cyber criminal could also simulate user typing and navigate to any page and insert any transaction.

At some point, manufacturers must create "secure" keyboards which could encrypt activity from the physical keyboard to the secure driver. With a secure keyboard, a compromised driver would be unable to compromise data. The data would have been encrypted before arriving at the computer.

Assuming a secure browser gets past the first challenge, the secure browser application will quickly become the attack vector of choice for the cyber criminal. There are several avenues available to the skilled attacker. The easiest is to simply inject code into the secure browser. Once injected all encrypted keystrokes would be visible as the browser decrypts them before sending them to the web server, now the browser is the man-in-the-middle. The developers responsible for creating the browser would need to be highly skilled in detecting and preventing the injection of the application.

Even if the browser is hardened against injection, it could still fall to a direct memory attack. Without touching the application or the driver, the attacker could simply read memory locations where decryption occurs. The only real protection from that type of attack must come from chip makers. Chip makers must provide protected memory space for these types of sensitive applications. A direct memory attack could be an issue even at the driver level mentioned earlier.

The developer of the secure browser also needs to worry about phishing attacks. Even with the data encrypted from the keyboard all the way to the application, credentials must be decrypted before being sent to the web server. Even if the secure browser is not susceptible to browser helper objects and the like, it is still subject to credential loss via man-in-the-middle attacks. Perhaps a well-crafted browser could further encrypt the data to the web server underneath the SSL session. With additional encryption, an interception by the attacker would result in the capture of encrypted credentials which are useless as long as they cannot be replayed.

As you can see, this technology is extremely complex. Mistakes at the drawing board can leave your users unprotected. When investigating this new technology, at minimum use anti-key logger testers such as those by FirewallLeakTester.com.[98] For a full-scale test, you should engage in a 3rd party to test the application for you, since it's likely to be outside your company's expertise.

This type of technology appears to be the proper long term direction. Still, it will take adoption by clients, along with cooperation of hardware manufacturers, to make this the winning technology.

---

98. Firewall Leak Tester. http://www.firewallleaktester.com/aklt.htm.

Terms

Binder – A tool used to combine, or bind, two or more EXE files into one single EXE file.

Code Obfuscation – The process where the binary of the malicious program undergoes various transformations to make it undetectable by anti-virus products.

HIPS – Host Based Intrusion Prevention System, a piece of software on the host that monitors the network and systems for malicious behavior. A HIPS application can automatically intervene in real-time.

NOP – No Operation, an assembly language instruction that does nothing.

Offset – In assembly language, the number of address locations from the base address.

Packer – A tool that compresses a piece of malware and creates a decompression program bound to the compressed malware.

PDF – Portable Document Format, it is a file format created by Adobe Systems in 1992. PDF files are used for document exchange.

Pseudocode – A compact and informal high-level description of a computer program.

Register – a small amount of memory on the CPU of a computer

VBS – Visual Basic Scripting Edition, a script language whose syntax makes it appear to be a subset of Microsoft's Visual Basic programming language.

CHAPTER 16 Epilogue

"The time has come," the walrus said, "to talk of many things: Of shoes and ships - and sealing wax - of cabbages and kings"

- Lewis Carroll (Alice's Adventures in Wonderland)

Unfortunately, time has come for this author to wrap this book up. Hopefully, you have journeyed safely to this point. While you may find the information presented in this book unpleasant, it's a fact of life. It is your job to take this knowledge and move your organization forward. Now that the magician's tricks have been revealed on both sides of the fence, you should be better prepared.

There is a price to pay for having a portal on the Internet, especially one that provides financial services. Defending that portal comes at a price. If the price is too high, you have two choices. Either stop playing the game, or change the rules. If you choose to stop playing the game, untold amounts of revenue may pass you by. That's probably not the proper choice. Fortunately, you can change the rules by fighting the cyber criminal with new technology, new tactics and new strategies. Ultimately, you must optimize your protection and squeeze every advantage out of the tools you acquire. The optimization that must occur at your organization is not a one time optimization either, nor is it yearly; it's on going daily evaluation and tweaking of your systems. You will make mistakes, you will spend some money incorrectly, but at the end of the day the fraud loss numbers will prove your success.

That leads us to one critical piece that was not mentioned in this tome, metrics. Metrics may be the buzzword for the 21st century; however for fraud they are essential. You, like the skilled juggler, will have many balls in the air at one time and as such it is essential that you know which tool sets are weakening at what points in time. This knowledge will allow you to shore those gaps up with new tools or techniques before the tool falls apart, or it will allow you to quickly identify useless technology and steer clear of similar systems in the future.

As a technologist the one thing I truly hate are meetings. Quite frankly, any meeting with more than three or four people typically becomes nonproductive. As a company, however, you must come together under a common banner to fight fraud. Daily meetings with your compliance groups, fraud groups, AML groups, information security and technology groups must occur. Speed and flexibility are essential, both in detection and implementation of technology. If you are a member of one of the unfortunate financial firms experiencing more of a hemorrhage than a bleed from fraud, then executive sponsorship is a must. The group tasked with fighting fraud must have not only the right people in it, but it must be able to tap any member of the firm for help at any time, as well as additional funds and decision making authority. If your firm is in the middle of a large loss, you can't wait several minutes for your fraud team to call out to someone to get permission to take a security, or in a doomsday scenario your trading system, offline. The decision must be made in the trenches to preserve your firm's best interests.

One thing firms don't like to do is share information; however with fraud the enemy is common. It is not a competitive advantage to withhold information. If several of your peers fall or have public incidences, you can be sure that customers will question your security and it will impact your bottom line. There are several organizations in place today that share information, and a simple call to your peers will likely reveal a lot to you, so pick up that phone.

It is this author's sincere hope that you now have some new-found knowledge, that you can now look at the latest technology and techniques with healthy skepticism. Remember, before you attempt to answer a problem, you must first know the question. By knowing the question, you can leap ahead of your peers. When searching for technology, always attempt to view it from the other side. Think how much time and effort it would take to circumvent. Layering ok and pretty good technologies will build you a defense that is greater than the sum of its parts. Just make sure you use the minimum number of layers to provide the maximum amount of protection.

I hope that you have a good grasp of what the cyber criminals are doing. They make mistakes just as you will. It's through these mistakes that one side can get the upper hand. The cyber criminal's goals are similar to yours; move as fast as you can, it doesn't have to be perfect it just has to work. From a targeting perspective, you just have to be harder to crack than your peers; unless you are the biggest fish in the ocean the cyber criminals will be content with softer targets rather than waste time on you.

Hopefully your journey through this book has been not only eye opening but one that has allowed you to think out of the box.

By the time you get to the end of this book, you're probably asking the questions, "Does the author conduct his financial transactions online?" and "How does he protect himself?" The answer is yes, I conduct about 99% of all my transactions online. I have purchased just about everything I own, with the exception of food, online. I do it because, ultimately, there is zero risk to me. My credit cards cover fraud losses so there is no reason not to transact online. As far as my protections, well, I'm probably more paranoid than most, though I wouldn't call it paranoia. I would call it, being as safe as technology will allow. The system I use to conduct all my transactions consists of a stripped down and hardened Windows XP virtual machine running Trend Internet Security Pro, along with Sana Securities Primary Response Safe-Connect, Xploit Prevention Labs LinkScanner and Previx's PrevixCSI. When my VM closes, the VM reverts back to its original state committing nothing to disk. While these products have obvious workarounds, remember the lesson on layering your security from earlier in this book. By layering technologies, I force the cyber criminal look for a common hole to get past all this pieces. It's highly unlikely that would occur. Is it possible? Yes. Is it probable today? Not likely.

So in closing the most important lessons of this book

- Reconnaissance of your enemy is key; know your enemy and what he is capable of
- Use surveillance to prepare for the future, what's theoretical today will be mainstream tomorrow
- Form fast moving tactical squads that meet daily
- Get executive buy-in and make sure you are supported with adequate resources
- Reach out to researchers and your peers in your industry
- Develop metrics to measure your success. They may not be perfect but slightly inaccurate numbers are better than out right guesses
- Deploy layered and diverse technologies; there is no single magic bullet. Remember, speed is better than perfection
- Educate your client base and your employees
- Be flexible, always adapt and change as required, there is no one time or quick fix

Of course, as the author, I'll put in a shameless plug for my own web site: www.efraudonline.com

APPENDIX A Analyzing Malware

To expand your company's ability to fight malicious code, you should learn how to analyze the various bots, worms and trojans that will attack your clients. Analyzing malware is not for the faint of heart. Typically, one or two people in your organization will specialize in performing this analysis. A great analyst will often have a solid programming background and the ability to read assembly language.

Code analysis involves not only reverse-engineering and code analysis, but the ability to look at behavioral aspects of the malware you are analyzing. There are numerous classes that can help you get started, or you can get the basics by looking at the various tools and taking a crack at it yourself. Listed below are tools the author of this book frequently relies on.

Tools for looking at changes to the computer

- System Monitor – System monitor is built into the Microsoft Windows operating systems and allows a quick and easy way to view various resources on the computer.

- Process Explorer – Process explorer is another tool built-into Windows that allows you to view running processes. While this tool won't find hidden processes it's still useful in this day and age.

- RegShot[99] – This tool can show you registry keys that have changed before and after a piece of malware has infected your PC.

Tools for reverse engineering the malware

- IDA Pro[100] – IDA Pro is a Windows/Linux multi-processor disassembler and debugger. It is an absolute must have.

- OllyDbg[101] – OllyDbg is an assembler level analyzing debugger with emphasis on binary code analysis. This tool allows you to analyze malware without source code.

- OllyDump[102] – OllyDump is a plug-in for dumping a running process to disk.

- OllyScript[103] – OllyScript is a plug-in that allows you to automate OllyDbg by writing scripts. It's not a necessity, but a nice tool when you become proficient in it.

- LordPE Deluxe – This tool allows you to view the parts of a portable execution (PE) file, dump them from memory, analyze them, etc. It's an all around great tool.

99. RegShot. http://regshot.blog.googlepages.com/regshot.

100. IDA Pro. http://hex?rays.com/idapro/.

101. OllyDbg. http://www.ollydbg.de/.

102. OllyDump. http://www.openrce.org/downloads/details/108/olly-dump.

103. OllyScript. http://www.openrce.org/downloads/details/106/olly-script.

Tools for building a sandbox to analyze the malware in

- VMWare[104] – VMWare allows you to build a virtual machine that you can infect to do analysis. Some malware now checks to see if it is running in VMWare to make it more difficult to analyze.

- Truman[105] – Truman can build an isolated environment to analyze malware. It also provides a virtual Internet for the malware to interact with. Because it runs on native hardware, it doesn't suffer from the VMWare issues that occur when malware has VMWare detection routines built in.

Tools for analyzing the web site with the malicious code

- Malzilla[106] – Malzilla allows you to explore malicious web pages. It also allows you to set your own user agent and referrer. Plus it can use proxies. It shows you the full source of the web page you are visiting and all the HTTP headers. It even has the ability to use various decoders to attempt to de-obfuscate JavaScript.

104.VMWare. http://www.vmware.com.
105.Truman. http://www.secureworks.com/research/tools/index.html.
106.Malzilla. http://malzilla.sourceforge.net.

Tools for watching the network

- NetCat[107] – Netcat reads and writes data across network connections and it can be scripted. It has many abilities, including port scanning and dumping of transmitted and received data.

- Honeyd[108] – Honeyd allows you to create virtual hosts on a network. You can configure these virtual hosts to run arbitrary services. They can appear to be running certain operating systems.

107.NetCat. http://netcat.sourceforge.net.
108.Honeyd. http://www.honeyd.org.

APPENDIX B Security Resources

Below is a list of security resources on the web. Some are very well known, while others have small followings. This list is not intended to be complete, nor is this list a recommendation of sites. For any site that didn't make the list, it certainly wasn't intentional. While the author would have liked to give you a summary of each, space did not allow, anyway exploration is always more fun than being told.

Computer Security News

Computer Crime Research Center
http://www.crime-research.org

Dark Reading
http://www.darkreading.com

eWeek
http://www.eweek.com/c/b/Security/

Personal Blog of Space Rogue
http://www.hackernews.com

SecurityFocus}
http://www.securityfocus.com

Security News Portal
http://www.securitynewsportal.com

Computer Standards

The Center for Internet Security
http://www.cisecurity.org/

Computer Emergency Response Team
http://www.cert.org

Nist Computer Security Division – Computer
Security Resource Center
http://csrc.nist.gov/

Intelligence

MyNetWatchman
http://www.mynetwatchman.com

National Cyber-Forensics & Training Alliance
http://www.ncfta.net

Team Cymru
http://www.cymru.com

Reporting of Computer Crimes

Internet Crime Complaint Center
http://www.ic3.gov/

Technical Information

2600: The Hacker Quarterly
http://www.2600.com

AntiOnline
http://www.antionline.com

Bruce Schneier's Web Site
http://www.schneier.com

Dis Org Crew
http://www.dis.org/

Hackers Blog
http://ha.ckers.org

Hackers Center
http://www.hackerscenter.com

HackPhreak
http://www.hackphreak.org

Happy Hacker Digests
http://www.happyhacker.org

Information System Security
http://www.infosyssec.com

Insecure.Org
http://insecure.org

LØpht Heavy Industries
http://www.l0pht.com

Microsoft Security Central
http://www.microsoft.com/security/
default.mspx

Phrack
http://www.phrack.com

SANS Institute
http://www.sans.org

Security Haven
http://www.securityhaven.com

UGN Security
http://www.undergroundnews.com

Web Application Security Consortium
http://www.webappsec.org

Training/Conferences

BlackHat
http://www.blackhat.com

DefCon
http://www.defcon.org

RSA Conference
http://www.rsaconference.com

Vulnerability Tracking

Common Vulnerabilities and Exposure
http://cve.mitre.org

Nist National Vulnerabiltiy Database
http://nvd.nist.gov/

www.ingramcontent.com/pod-product-compliance
Lightning Source LLC
LaVergne TN
LVHW022259060326
832902LV00020B/3173